DECISIONS
WITHOUT
HIERARCHY

DECISIONS WITHOUT HIERARCHY

FEMINIST INTERVENTIONS IN ORGANIZATION THEORY AND PRACTICE

KATHLEEN P. IANNELLO

ROUTLEDGE • NEW YORK & LONDON

Published in 1992 by

Routledge
An imprint of Routledge, Chapman and Hall, Inc.
29 West 35 Street
New York, NY 10001

Published in Great Britain by

Routledge
11 New Fetter Lane
London EC4P 4EE

Library of Congress Cataloging in Publication Data

Iannello, Kathleen P., 1954–
    Decisions without hierarchy : feminist interventions in
organization theory and practice / Kathleen P. Iannello.
        p.   cm.
    Includes bibliographical references and index.
    ISBN 0-415-90428-5   ISBN 0-415-90429-3
    1. Organizational sociology—United States. 2. Feminist theory.
3. Decision-making—United States—Case Studies. I. Title.
HM131.I284 1992
305.42'01—dc20   92-12562
                                                                                          CIP

British Library cataloguing in publication data also available

I would like to dedicate this book to the
memory of Dr. Frank Sim, whose
insights and thorough knowledge of
organizations guided my work beyond
his death in 1985.

Contents

Acknowledgments

I would like to thank the multitude of people who helped bring this project to completion. Foremost among them are the women of the peace group, health collective, and business group who allowed a stranger to observe meetings as well as consume their time with unending questions.

Next, a special thanks goes to family members who provided the necessary at-home support. First among them is my spouse, Terry Dalton, assisted by our sons, Brendan and Trevin Dalton, as well as a coalition of other Daltons and Iannellos.

Another round of thanks goes to Robert Friedman, Jim Eisenstein, Larry Spence, Marylee Taylor, and Nancy Love of Penn State for their advice with the first draft of this document. Encouragement in the revision process came from many of my former colleagues at Dartmouth College, particularly Lynn Mather, Frank Smallwood, and Dick Winters, my Dartmouth students, and John P. Burke at the University of Vermont.

I am indebted to many at Gettysburg College for their support of this project. Jean Potuchek, Liliane Floge, and the women of the feminist research discussion group contributed insightful comments and always kept their doors open for impromptu consultation. Jamee Conover, Sue Welch, and my student assistant, Keith Stirewalt, did a first-rate job on the editing of the manuscript. I am also grateful to my colleagues in Political Science for their continual encouragement and also for the financial support provided by my department and the Gettysburg College Research and Professional Development Fund.

Further, I would like to thank Pam Regis of Western Maryland College for suggesting the title of the book; Ginny Story for the index; the editors at Routledge for their interest and guidance; Hester Eisenstein for the inspiration and direction her work has provided; and Wendy Sarvasy for starting it all.

Preface

Decisions Without Hierarchy is part of a growing literature that assesses the contributions of feminism over the past twenty years—a literature some call the study of feminist interventions.[1] Specifically, this study intends to address, from a feminist perspective, a series of questions regarding decision making and organization structure. For example, why do we assume decision making must be hierarchical? Under what circumstances can non-hierarchy be maintained? What are the benefits and costs that result from non-hierarchical process? And what are its possible applications?

Part I of this book explores feminist interventions in organization theory by considering the starting points of organization theory and feminist theory, as well as the points at which their lines of inquiry converge. For example, organization theory begins from the world as it is, a world in which hierarchies organize all aspects of life. It does not ask whether hierarchies should exist, but simply how they can be run more smoothly. Feminist theory, on the other hand, begins from the world as it ought to be, one in which gender hierarchies have been eliminated; thus, it assumes the possibility for fundamental social change.

Part II explores feminist interventions in organization practice. Included are three case studies of feminist organizations in a small New England city. These studies provide examples of feminist practice that yield what can be termed *modified consensus*.

Modified consensus is both a method of decision making and a form of organization. It is not, as many would assume, a form of consensual structure that has inevitably given in to hierarchy. Instead, modified consensus falls outside such categorizations and contributes to new understandings about the ways in which non-hierarchical structure works.

While retaining the practice and spirit of consensual process, modified consensus at the same time efficiently meets internal and external environmental demands placed on organizations. This is path-breaking, because the concepts of consensus and efficiency have not often been viewed as compatible. Decision by consensus means that all members of an organization have the opportunity to discuss matters of policy until a decision acceptable to everyone is reached. It is this process of discussion, delay, and non-voting that has led to charges of inefficiency.

Modified consensus responds to the problem of efficiency through outward (not downward) delegation of routine decisions to those in the organization with particular skill and knowledge in what all members of the organization determine to be routine areas. But critical decisions, those that determine the overall path and goals, are retained for the entire membership and are arrived at consensually. This is very different from decision making in hierarchies, in which critical decisions are made by the few at the top of the organization. It is thus with the role of hierarchy in organizations that this study begins.

NOTES

1. See Hester Eisenstein, *Gender Shock* (Boston: Beacon, 1991), and also Sophie Watson ed., *Playing the State: Australian Feminist Interventions* (Verso and Sydney: Allen & Unwin, 1990).

PART ONE

O N E

The Starting Point of Organization Theory

Whether public or private, government or family, school or church, organizations have a significant influence on everything we do. "The development of organizations is the principle mechanism by which, in a highly differentiated society, it is possible to 'get things done,' to achieve goals beyond the reach of the individual."[1] Because of this, the study of organizations in society has received much attention. From the philosophers of ancient Greece to the corporate heads of the twentieth century, the question of how to organize in order to achieve specific goals and purposes has provoked interest.

Within the body of modern literature that has come to be known as organization theory, many studies have had great impact on our views of the organizations around us. Theorists such as Frederick Taylor, Elton Mayo, Chester Barnard, and Robert Merton, to name a few, conducted the early studies, which tended to focus on the structure and function of organizations. Perhaps none had so great an impact as the German sociologist Robert Michels, who was among the first to focus on the growth of public bureaucracy.

Michels in particular dealt specifically with the problems of democratic theory, in 1911 publishing *Political Parties*, an intensive study of the German Social Democratic Party. That seminal work altered the landscape of organization theory in a way that today's political scientists and sociologists often fail to recognize. Michels's now famous "iron law of oligarchy"—that oligarchy is inherent in or synonymous with organization—is seen as a statement not just about the nature of a political party in pre–World War I Germany, but about the nature of all organizations, whether party, trade union, or church. His formulation excludes, in no uncertain terms, possibilities for egalitarian organization, even among the most ideologically committed:

> Democracy leads to oligarchy, and necessarily contains an oligarchical nucleus. In making this assertation it is far from the author's intention to pass moral judgment upon any political party or any system of government, to level an accusation of hypocrisy. The law that it is an essential characteristic of all human aggregates to constitute cliques and sub-classes is like every other sociological law, beyond good and evil.[2]

For Michels, oligarchy seemed simply to be a result of human nature. He was not alone in this conclusion; the work of his contemporaries, Gaetano Mosca and Vilfredo Pareto, provided evidence to support his claims.[3]

Through empirical research Michels observed that while egalitarian organizations were often a goal, that goal became displaced by other organizational concerns. According to Michels, the German Socialist party had every reason to succeed in its attempts toward a more participatory form of organization. It was a party that fought for adult suffrage, free speech, and popular participation. Yet it could not avoid the internal development of a self-interested ruling class. Michels calls it "a universally applicable social law" that every organization has a need for division of labor, and that as soon as these divisions are created, so too are special interests.[4] These interests develop conflicts with the interests of the collectivity and "undergo transformation" into distinct classes. A "ruling class" then emerges, holding the advantages of superior knowledge and information. It can secure its position by controlling the formal means of communication, as in organizing group activities.[5]

In addition, Michels explains that the other classes frequently display incompetence by not participating, attending meetings, or voting as much as they might, thus reinforcing the position of the elite. As the organization develops, the elite becomes more interested in maintaining its own position than in achieving the original goals of the organization. External challenges from other organizations help to solidify this position, causing the original goals of the organization to become displaced and making survival into an end in itself. Maintaining the organization, and one's elite position within it, becomes a goal of great personal importance. "The party is created as a means to secure an end. Having, however, become an end in itself, endowed with aims and interests of its own, it undergoes detachment, from the teleological point of view, from the class it represents."[6]

Citing historical evidence for his claims, Michels developed a pessimistic attitude toward the possibilities for success of any democratic experiment.[7] He began to consider the role of charismatic leadership in organizing the masses behind a political cause. This is what eventually led to his fascination with the Italian fascist leader Benito Mussolini.

While Michels's work has not gone uncriticized, little evidence has been provided to challenge his theory. Seymour Lipset, Martin Trow, and James Coleman's work, *Union Democracy,* provides the one notable exception to the "iron law" in the example of the democratically run International Typographical Union (ITU). However, even these authors hold a dim view of the chances for democracy in other organizations.

> We have shown that there is much more variation in the internal organization of associations than the notion of an iron law of oligarchy would imply, but nevertheless, the implications of our analysis for democratic organizational politics are almost as pessimistic as those postulated by Robert Michels.[8]

Many of the conditions that enable the ITU to be democratic in nature are difficult to duplicate. Certain factors were present when the international union was organized: for example, strong local union organizations already existed, which were able to resist the efforts toward a highly centralized structure. The organization was created from the bottom up, not from the top down. In addition, the printers had a strong identification and pride in their craft, which made them more likely to want to participate in the organization. These patterns persisted after the ITU developed, safeguarding against the oligarchic tendencies of bureaucratic structure.[9]

Perhaps the greatest criticism of Michels's work has come from socialists and Marxists. They argue that Michels's theory is based on a society in which economic class divisions already exist; the organization Michels studied simply mirrored the rest of society. The Marxist argument suggests that in a society where economic status is held constant, egalitarian organization has a much greater chance for success. This viewpoint will be discussed below within the context of critical perspectives in organization theory.

Another criticism of Michels's work focuses on his argument regarding the divergence in interests between the ruling classes and the ruled. The evidence suggests that Michels may have misread the Social Democratic party's shift to the right prior to World War I as an initiative of the ruling class. In fact, this shift appears to have come from the party members first, implying that the ruling class had not "deflected" the organization from the "goals and the beliefs of the members."[10] This information offers at least some reason to believe that the link between the rulers and the ruled was not as weak as Michels believed.

Despite suggestions that Michels's study may be overly pessimistic with respect to possibilities for democracy, the "iron law" has become what can be called the "dominant" perspective of organizational theory.[11] Other "critical" perspectives have not been as widely recognized. For both the rational or scientific management model of organization theory and the natural or human relations model, hierarchy is an unquestioned structural characteristic of organizations.

Frederick Taylor was one of the earliest proponents of *rational* theory, publishing *The Principles of Scientific Management* in 1911, which emphasized routine methods, logic in planning, and suppression of the "irrational" tendencies of workers. Rational planning was viewed as the task of a managerial class, which would establish the direction of the organization and design and operate the administrative machinery necessary to accomplish the job. Later theorists such as Chester Barnard and Herbert Simon began to stress information and communication within the administrative structure, but still supported the basic view of rational planning.

The *natural* or human relations model of organization theory, led by Elton Mayo, began to explore the more "human" side of organizations, focusing on what had been considered irrational elements of human behavior. Through this kind of exploration a theory of "informal" as well as "formal" organization developed. The informal organization was the social network formed among workers or organization members—the unwritten rules, attitudes, or behaviors that influenced the productivity and environment of workers.

This distinction led to attempts to mediate hierarchy by developing more participatory types of management or by eliminating levels of management, in order to get more worker/member input. This style of management is associated with the work of Chris Argyris, Rensis Likert, and Douglas McGregor, to name a few.[12] However, the discovery of the informal aspects of organizations did not alter the distinction between the managerial/rational class and the worker/irrational class. It did not alter the view that hierarchy was needed to accomplish organization goals.

Despite this dominant view, others continue to study hierarchy as a less desirable structure, one that fosters conflict among organization members and promotes domination and control of members by organization leaders. Supporters of this view argue that hierarchy often impedes the attainment of organization goals, because it promotes competition to the extent that competition becomes a goal in itself. This "critical" perspective does not view hierarchy as inevitable. Instead, it argues that alternatives to hierarchy are possible if we study it as the outcome of the values, norms, and ideologies of the host society.

This critical view is the product of yet another strain of organization theory, known as the *open systems* model. This model focuses on the relationship between organizations and their environment.

> That a system is open means not simply that it engages in interchanges with the environment, but that this interchange is an essential factor underlying the system's viability.[13]

Theorists such as Victor Thompson and Charles Perrow, Paul R. Lawrence, and Gay W. Lorsch developed the structural contingency model, which "treated organizations as open systems subject to uncertainty arising from both environment and technology."[14] Working from this view of organizations, others such as Graeme Salaman, J. Kenneth Benson, and John W. Myer and Brian Rowan have been able to consider the impact of societal values on the structure and operation of organizations, focusing particularly on power relationships.

One significant aspect of the critical perspective has been the attention given to economic systems and their effect on organization structure. In the case of capitalism, it is argued that values underlying the market system support and promote hierarchy in other types of organizations. Capitalism creates class distinctions, introducing the notion of a ruling class or elite and the perception of a need to maintain power at the top of an organization. As Mary Zey-Ferrell and Michael Aiken explain: "Bureaucratic control techniques of hierarchy and division of labor result as much from the need to impose labor discipline as from abstract notions of rational work efficiency."[15] This need to impose discipline, it is argued, comes from values related to the market system.

Before these perspectives can be considered in relation to feminist theory and practice, however, it is important to gain an understanding of the terms *organization, hierarchy,* and *bureaucracy.*

ORGANIZATIONS

While the literature of organization theory provides much discussion of types of organizations, it is sometimes vague regarding the meaning of this basic term. Bureaucracy, hierarchy, and oligarchy are examples of terms used in defining certain types of organizations, but the term *organization* must first be considered on its own.

Max Weber defined an organization as a system of continuous purposive activity "with specialization of function, administrative staff devoted to such . . . activity and intent to maintain the existence of the specialized activities."[16] The use of the word "administrative" has often been taken to imply that hierarchy or bureaucracy is necessary for an organization to survive and achieve goals. While evidence suggests that this is true for many organizations, a definition of the concept of organization should allow for as many variations as possible. Administration brings to mind formal structure that may not be present in some organizations that take care of leadership responsibilities in a much more informal manner.

For example, the women's consciousness-raising groups of the 1960s were often said to lack structure. Instead, informal leadership often developed through the personal strength of individual members. While this could result in "tyranny," or unaccountable leadership, as Jo Freeman points out,[17] such leadership does not constitute "formal" administration as defined by Weber. Yet these groups were certainly "organizations." Weber's definition thus excludes from study structures that offer important contributions to an understanding of how organizations can and do function. As an alternative, one might define organizations as systems of continuous, purposive, goal-oriented activity involving two or more people.

W. Richard Scott, in his book *Organizations,* takes a comprehensive approach to the concept. He offers three different definitions compatible with the three different approaches to the study of organizations discussed earlier. The first definition recalls the rational systems approach, viewing the organization as "a collectivity oriented to the pursuit of relatively specific goals and exhibiting a relatively highly formalized social structure."[18] By contrast, the natural systems perspective views organizations as "organic" systems attempting to maintain themselves as a system. The emphasis here is on informal structure. Thus the organization is defined as "a collectivity whose participants are little affected by the formal structure or official goals but who share a common interest in the survival of the system and who engage in collective activities, informally structured, to secure this end."[19]

Both the rational and natural systems approaches fail to account for environmental influences on organizations; or in other words, they are closed systems. Thus, Scott's third category, the open systems approach, focuses on such influences viewing organizations as variable in nature. The organization thus becomes "a coalition of shifting interest groups that developed goals by negotiation; the structure of the coalition, its activities, and its outcomes are strongly influenced by environmental factors."[20]

In consideration of these three perspectives it is now generally agreed that, as Marshall Meyer aptly puts it, the argument is "closed, on the side of openness."[21] Theorists have widely accepted the open systems definition, viewing organizations as coalitions not rigidly linked in a unitary hierarchy.[22] Instead, the organization subgroups are seen as "loosely coupled," in the sense that each can respond to changes in other groups. Yet degrees of autonomy among the groups may vary a great deal.

In addition, as the natural systems perspective points out, "the normative structure of an organization is only loosely coupled with its behavioral structure," meaning that formal rules and informal actions may not constitute a perfect fit. In other words, "rules do not always govern actions: each exhibits a capacity for autonomous action."[23] Theorists differ on the implications for efficiency. For rational systems theorists, "loose coupling" tends to mean bad management, an inefficient means of attaining organizational goals. Open system theorists disagree, arguing that loosely coupled systems may increase efficiency in certain situations because of their highly adaptive nature. Further, by continually obtaining resources from the environment, open systems are capable of "self-maintenance." Closed systems are more likely to become static because they do not derive a constant flow of energy and resources from the environment.

The open systems approach argues that different environments can place different demands on organizations, especially in the case of rapidly changing technologies and market conditions. Thus "organizations whose internal features best match the demands of their environments will achieve the best adaptation"[24]: an argument labeled *contingency theory.* Within this open-systems theory, the *natural selection* model argues that "environments differentially select certain types of organizations for survival on the basis of fit between organizational forms and environmental characteristics."[25] In contrast, the *resource dependence* model stresses adaptation: "subunits of the organization . . . scan the relevant environment for opportunities and threats, formulate strategic responses and adjust organizational structure accordingly."[26] Thus, managers attempt to maximize control over the organization by maximizing the opportunities that present themselves in the environment. According to the open systems perspective, the organization within the environment undergoes an ongoing process of adaptation: the environment influences the organization and the organization can attempt to take advantage of the environment. This interdependence is the major focus of the open systems perspective.

While this definition of organizations provides a broad base for organizational study, it still fails to consider the environment as an entire *society* in which prevailing values, ideologies, or political ideals have important and pervasive influences on organizations. The critical perspective discussed earlier provides this view, by focusing on "the relationship between internal organizational structures, processes and ideologies and the society in which they exist."[27] For example, rather than examining the impact on organizations of fluctuating market conditions, the critical perspective considers the nature of the market itself—capitalist or socialist—and the impact on organizations of the value systems underlying them.

In addition, the critical perspective considers a history of organizations within the larger society. The tendency of the open systems as well as the rational and natural systems perspectives is to ignore the historical development of organizations. The example provided by Lipset, Trow, and Coleman in *Union Democracy* underscores the importance of looking at historical roots. As mentioned earlier, historical developments offered the key to understanding how the trade union could operate in a democratic fashion. Yet one must recognize that historical approaches have tended to study organizations primarily from an administrative or "top-down" view, when consideration of how the organization looks from the bottom up is at the very least of equal importance.

The critical perspective thus focuses on the significance of what have been termed the "nonrational human, institutional, and societal elements."[28] As Zey-Ferrell and Aiken point out:

We should not merely acknowledge the nonrational and irrational aspects of organizations and then rush to analyze the rational aspects but ... our analysis should center on these nonrational and irrational aspects, because these are the ways organizations operate in the real world.[29]

The critical perspective thus contributes significantly to the development of a definition of organizations that is able to incorporate a feminist perspective. First, by focusing on the environment as a whole, the critical perspective allows for the study of the impact of societal values on organization structure. Patriarchy may be analyzed as one such condition under which organizations exist. While theorists within the critical perspective have considered the impact of domination as it is fostered by capitalism, the question of domination as it is fostered by patriarchy has only begun to be explored.

Secondly, the critical perspective, in considering variables in organizational analysis that were previously considered "irrational," offers a more inclusive approach. By focusing on the historical development of organizations, one may begin to move away from a "universalistic" approach toward what is unique.[30] This allows for the serious consideration of power relations within organizations, not just from the viewpoint of administration, but from that of all organization members.

From a feminist standpoint one might begin to address the connection between patriarchy and power. Does power always mean domination in organizations? Are there other understandings of power? In one analysis of power, the critical perspective put forth the following questions:

How did the existing relationship originate? Which classes and groups are benefited by the existing relationship? How does the dominant coalition maintain and perpetuate its control? What are the consequences of the present distribution of power in the organization for present society and for future generations?[31]

It is clear that the critical perspective adds another dimension to the meaning of "organization." This does not discount the wealth of information provided by the rational, natural systems, and open systems perspectives. However, what is learned from these perspectives is only part of the organizational picture; it lacks the information provided by the critical perspective with respect to historical development and societal values. By considering all four perspectives, one may define organizations as follows: organizations are systems of continuous, purposive, goal-oriented activity, involving two or more people, which exist within, and to some extent are affected by, a value system provided by the larger societal environment.

HIERARCHY AND BUREAUCRACY

Like many of the concepts related to organizations, hierarchy is often undefined or confused with other concepts in the literature. The term is often used as synonymous with organization,[32] yet it is also often confused with bureaucracy. Previous discussion regarding the definition of the term "organization" provides some clarification on this point. However, the concept of bureaucracy requires further discussion.

Bureaucracy is most simply defined as "the existence of some kind of specialized administrative staff."[33] One of the best known definitions is that of Max Weber, who defines bureaucracy through the use of a list of characteristics:

> A fixed division of labor among participants, a hierarchy of offices, a set of general rules which govern performance, a separation of personal from official property and rights, selection of personnel on the basis of technical qualifications and employment viewed as a career by participants.[34]

As Weber indicates, bureaucracy is a concept that encompasses many organizational characteristics, of which hierarchy is one. However, it can be argued that hierarchy is the key component of bureaucracy, around which channels of authority, systems of communication, and performance guidelines have developed. Evidence of this is provided through the discussion of hierarchy within the dominant perspective of organizations. For instance, Michels argues that in any organization division of labor comes first; then the mechanisms necessary to support and sustain such division develop to such an extent that their maintenance becomes the overriding goal in itself. Within this discussion it is important to consider the possibility that organizations may develop rules and operating procedures without developing hierarchy. If hierarchy is considered to be the defining element of bureaucracy, then such organizations do not constitute bureaucracies.

Certainly, Weber considered non-bureaucratic organizations in his discussion of administrative forms, but only in contrasting the development of modern administrative organizations with the patrimonial systems from which they developed. A patrimonial system is defined as "an estate or production organization governed by a ruler-owner who relies for assistance on a variety of dependents, ranging from slaves to sons, in managing the enterprise."[35] This was obviously an authoritarian, patriarchical arrangement. Yet Weber's discussion serves to point out that the patrimonial system, however rigid in its actual operation, was an informal one, in which the rules were not written and roles within the system could change at any time according to the whims of the ruler-owner. Modern bureaucratic structure, on the other hand, is formalized: jurisdictional areas are clearly specified within a hierarchy, whereas in patrimonial systems authority relations were based more on personal loyalties.

Weber's discussion thus suggests that formalized hierarchy is the key defining element of bureaucracy. In considering more egalitarian organizational forms, hierarchy must become an important focus. The question arises as to whether organizations can develop in non-hierarchical and therefore non-bureaucratic ways without imitating the informal structures of patrimonial systems. This is a question of importance to this study.

NOTES

1. W. Richard Scott, *Organizations* (Englewood Cliffs, N.J.: Prentice-Hall, 1981), p. 4.

2. Robert Michels, *Political Parties* (New York: The Free Press, 1962), p. 6.

3. Ibid., pp. 342–356. See also, Gaetano Mosca, *The Ruling Class,* (New York: McGraw-Hill, 1939), and Vilfredo Pareto, *The Ruling Class in Italy Before 1900* (New York: H. Fertig, 1974).

4. Ibid., p. 153.

5. Ibid., p. 16.

6. Ibid., p. 353.

7. Ibid., p. 355.

8. Seymour Martin Lipset, Martin A. Trow, and James S. Coleman, *Union Democracy* (Glencoe, Ill.: The Free Press, 1956), p. 405.

9. Ibid., p. 394.

10. Ibid., p. 30.

11. The terms *critical perspective* and *dominant perspective* are derived from the work of Mary Zey-Ferrell and Michael Aiken in their book *Complex Organizations: Critical Perspectives* (Glenview, Ill.: Scott, Foresman, and Co.).

12. See Chris Argyris, *Personality and Organization* (New York: Harper & Row, 1957); Rensis Likert, *New Patterns of Management* (New York: McGraw-Hill, 1961); and Douglas McGregor, *The Human Side of Enterprise* (New York: McGraw-Hill, 1960).

13. Scott, p. 102.

14. Zey-Ferrell and Aiken, p. 2.

15. Ibid., p. 4.
16. Scott, p. 57.
17. See Jo Freeman, *The Politics of Women's Liberation* (New York: Longman, 1975).
18. Scott, p. 21.
19. Ibid., p. 22.
20. Ibid., p. 23.
21. Marshall W. Meyer, *Environments and Organizations* (London: Jossey-Bass, 1987), p. 18.
22. Scott, p. 108.
23. Ibid., p. 108.
24. Ibid., p. 114.
25. Ibid., p. 115.
26. Ibid., p. 116.
27. Zey-Ferrell and Aiken, p. 3.
28. Ibid., p. 9.
29. Ibid., p. 10.
30. Ibid., p. 16.
31. Ibid., p. 17.
32. Larry D. Spence, "Prolegomena to a Communications Theory of Human Organizations" (Unpublished manuscript, Department of Political Science, University of California, Berkeley, January 1969), p. 8.
33. Scott, p. 24.
34. Ibid., p. 68.
35. Ibid.

T W O

Hierarchy

The concept of hierarchy was invented in the fifth century by Denys the Areopagite.[1] He used the term to define and describe an organizational structure based on the top-down delegation of power and determination of functions. This system derived from his religious beliefs; for the Greeks, *hierarchy* meant "sacred rule."[2] The word was also adopted to "denote the power given by Christ to his apostles and their successors to form and govern the church."[3] Later, Shakespeare defended the concept of hierarchy in his play *Troilus and Cressida* with the following famous passage: "Take but degree away, untune that string, and hark what discord follows."[4]

In the modern literature of organization theory, the term has been defined as "any system in which the distributions of power, privilege and authority are both systematic and unequal."[5] Power can be taken here to mean domination, while privilege implies a right, immunity, or benefit enjoyed by a particular person or a restricted group of persons. Authority can be defined as "legitimate" power, in which those subject to domination by others accept that domination as a legitimate arrangement. Given this use of these terms, a more specific definition of hierarchy results: "society arranged according to 'degree,' with power, privilege and authority varying together."[6]

Most other definitions of hierarchy have incorporated some variations of power, privilege, and authority, but have been more specific in describing the exact relationships between them. This has been particularly true of definitions coming from theorists ascribing to the rational systems point of view. Weber's definition of hierarchy states that each lower office is controlled and supervised by a higher one. Other rational systems theorists, such as James Mooney and A.C. Reiley and Luther Gulick and L. Urwick, emphasize the importance of coordination and specialization.[7] Coordination is the "vertical" arrangement, including the scalar principle, unity of command, span of control, and the exception principle. These categories warrant further explanation.

The scalar principle emphasizes hierarchical organization "in which all participants are linked into a single pyramidal structure of control relations."[8] Unity of command means that no organization members receive orders from more than one superior. Span of control means that no superior should have more subordinates than can be overseen, and the exception principle means that all routine matters are handled by subordinates, so that the superior is free to deal with "exceptional" situations. This is the distinction that Selznick later describes as that between "routine" versus "critical" decisions.[9]

Specialization refers more to the horizontal division of labor. This concept has two major elements: the departmentalization principle and the line-staff principle. The first is a method of organizing based on homogeneity of activity, whether of purpose, process, or clientele. The line-staff principle means that activities dealing with organization goals are line functions and that the staff is there to provide administrative support for those individuals engaged in those activities. Together, coordination as a vertical element and specialization as a horizontal element create the power, privilege, and authority relations within a hierarchy.

One important element missing from this configuration of hierarchy is communication. Some theorists believe this aspect to be of such importance that they define hierarchy as "centralized communication systems."[10] Whether hierarchy is defined as a communications system or not, the flow of information up and down the pyramidal structure forms an important aspect of power, privilege, and authority relationships. In most instances, the possession of information or knowledge constitutes power. It is the possession of information, on one hand, and the deprivation of it, on the other that keeps systems of domination in operation.

> Certain messages can travel in only one direction: Definitional messages (what is to be done, who is to do it, etc.) travel down the scale, operational messages (what was done, what happened, etc.) travel up the scale. Message priorities are based on positional origin, not

content. Further limits on message content are constrictive for lower ranks and permissive for upper ranks. Access to stored information is confined to upper ranks and denied lower ranks, etc.[11]

The relationship between information and hierarchy takes on interest in light of the question of efficiency. As Blau and Scott point out, "there appears to be a curvilinear relation between information-processing requirements and the utility of hierarchy."[12] In other words, if there is little information to be transmitted within an organization, there may be no particular advantages to hierarchy and some clear disadvantages, such as the costs of administrative overhead. As the volume of information increases, however, hierarchies can offer benefit in reducing transmission costs and ensuring coordination—up to a certain point. If the volume of information grows excessive, hierarchies become overloaded, and resources at the lowest levels of the organization are underutilized.[13]

Considering these factors, hierarchy can be defined as a vertical and horizontal system of domination with varying degrees of centralized communication. Within this system of domination, privilege and authority are determined by scalar position within the organization, not by the person holding the position. Once a person has held a position for an extended period of time, however, this distinction between individual and position becomes less clear. Informal leadership characteristics may or may not qualify a certain individual for a certain position within the hierarchy. Thus, a distinction should be made between domination and leadership. Domination can be characterized by the following factors:

a) the position of headship is maintained through an organized system and not by the spontaneous recognition of the individual contribution to the group goal; b) the group goal is arbitrarily chosen by the autocratic head in his own self-interest and is not internally determined; c) there is not really a *group* at all, since there is no sense of shared feeling or joint action; and d) there is in this process a wide social gap between the group members and the head, who strives to maintain this social distance as an aid to his coercion of the group through fear.[14]

The difference in organizational settings between leadership and domination is an important one. This is particularly true with regard to the development of more egalitarian forms of organization. Every organization faces the question of leadership. As mentioned earlier, organizations attempting to avoid hierarchical structure face a dilemma. Such organizations may wish to allow leadership to develop naturally out of the skills and interests of its members. However, there is a danger that certain members may gain positions of power within the organization without those positions being formalized. Once such individuals develop power there is no procedural means of removing them from the position. Yet if positions are formalized, the organization runs the risk of becoming a hierarchy—what it was attempting to avoid. This is a dilemma that will be discussed at greater length with regard to the three women's organizations studied herein.

In focusing on the question of whether more egalitarian forms of organization can exist, it is necessary to consider the relative costs and benefits of hierarchy. Theorists with the most positive view of hierarchy come primarily from the rational systems perspective. As one would expect, they view hierarchy as the most efficient means of attaining organization goals. The "essential elements" of the rational perspective are goal specificity and formalization. Specification of goals allows the organization to select among desired activities and design a specific organization structure to accomplish those desired tasks. Formalization means that "rules governing behavior are precisely and explicitly formulated."[15] Such rules attempt to make behavior predictable, in order to foster stable expectations and the conditions for rational planning.

A primary school of thought within this perspective is that of scientific management. This approach, mainly put forth by Frederick Taylor in 1911, sought to rationalize every activity of managers and workers in order to "produce the maximum output with the minimum input of energies and resources."[16] Taylor was attempting to rationalize the organization from the bottom up, while others, such as Henri Fayol, were developing another school of administrative principles to rationalize the organization from the top down.

Weber's theory of bureaucracy is also categorized within this rational perspective, though Weber himself was simply describing, not advocating, such a view. Given that coordination and specialization are key elements of hierarchy, it is not difficult to see how well Weber's position fits with the rational perspective. Hierarchy's benefits include providing the necessary structure for what is perceived to be efficient management. By specifying roles and coordinating tasks within the organization, more time is spent in working toward goals than in working out power and authority relations. This part of the organization is already a 'given'.[17]

Not only the rational systems theorists see benefits to hierarchy. Natural and open systems theorists emphasize benefits with regard to communication, but, again, these are viewed in terms of efficiency in information processing. Studies indicate that:

> The centralized structures more rapidly organize to solve the problems. Participants in peripheral positions send information to the center of the network, where a decision is made and sent out to the periphery. Furthermore, this pattern of organization tends to be highly stable once developed. In less centralized structures the organization problem is more difficult and observed interaction patterns are less stable, as well as less efficient.[18]

This statement raises questions concerning the concepts of centralization and decentralization with regard to hierarchy and organization.

CENTRALIZATION, DECENTRALIZATION, AND FRAGMENTATION

In the discussion of hierarchical versus non-hierarchical organization, consideration of top-down versus bottom-up styles of management merits importance. The terms *centralization, decentralization,* and *fragmentation* are often used to refer to one or the other of these arrangements. Centralization usually refers to the top-down arrangement; however, confusion often exists with regard to the association of decentralization with the bottom-up style. Decentralization and fragmentation are often confused and warrant further clarification.

Decentralization has commonly been described in the political science literature simply as delegation of authority from the center or top level to lower levels of an organization.[19] The degree to which decision-making authority can be pushed downward may relate directly to the life cycle of an organization. Organizations evolve, beginning as centralized structures and moving toward decentralization.[20] They are centralized at first due to the need to develop the path upon which the organization will embark. The determination of policy goals allows the organization to develop more of a similar mindset among members or personnel. This homogeneous outlook helps ensure that when authority is pushed downward, decisions made at lower levels are likely to be compatible with the overall direction of the organization. Centralization and determination of organizational pur-

pose also allow for distinctions to be made as to whether policy decisions are critical or routine.[21] Critical decisions are those that will
most clearly affect survival of the organization. Routine decisions are
made on a daily basis and are unlikely to alter significantly the organization's future.

This distinction between critical and routine decision making is
crucial to the implementation and maintenance of decentralization,
because it sets up the structure for maintaining authority at the center
of the organization while still allowing for delegation of responsibility
to lower levels. In a decentralized setting, critical decisions are reserved for those at the top level of the organization, while routine
decisions are delegated downward. This is thought to be useful for
at least two reasons. First, lower-level personnel who are delegated
responsibility deal with problems they are close to and have information about. They are assumed to have the resources needed to make
whatever the organization defines as effective decisions at this level.
Thus, decentralization allows for some degree of adaptation at lower
levels. Second, as Selznick's work indicates, executives who are freed
from routine decision making have more time to consider the larger
policy questions that will ultimately determine the direction of the organization.[22]

Yet even in the case of routine decisions, guidelines accompany the
delegation of authority. Such guidelines allow for some discretion by
personnel at lower levels, but may restrict the options or decisions
available. If this occurs to the extent that decisions are absolutely prescribed, the organization remains centralized. Such were the findings
of Herbert Kaufman's study of the Forest Service.[23] Although forest
rangers located in various parks were delegated authority to make
decisions, the types of decisions and the ways to implement them had
already been specified by the central authority. Thus, the organization was centralized.

In the course of events affecting organizations, it is possible for
routine decisions to become critical ones. Within a decentralized organization, the upper level or center should retain and exercise the
authority to recall responsibility it has delegated. If the upper level is
unable to do this, the organization is moving toward fragmentation.
Fragmentation can most clearly be identified when critical policy is
made at lower levels, shifting the direction of the organization without
guidance from upper levels.[24] Given these distinctions, decentralization can be defined as the delegation of authority from the center to
lower levels, with the following requirements: critical policy decisions

are reserved for the center while routine decisions are delegated to lower levels, and the center retains and is able to exercise the power to recall authority it has delegated.

TOWARD A CRITIQUE OF HIERARCHY

Unlike rational systems theorists, natural and open systems theorists perceive some of the costs of hierarchy along with the benefits. As alluded to above, there is a curvilinear relationship between information processing and the utility of hierarchy, in that in the case of only a low level of information or of too high a level, the costs of administration outweigh the benefits. In fact, as Scott points out, "It would be incorrect . . . to conclude that hierarchies are superior to more decentralized or egalitarian arrangements under all conditions."[25]

Natural and open systems theorists have shown that hierarchies impede work and can interfere with tasks presenting complex or ambiguous problems.[26] They impede work by stifling interaction among workers, as well as between workers and managers. Hierarchy undermines social support among organization members in that the workplace is formalized to the extent that "human" needs are not considered part of the process. Such a structure often reduces incentives for employees to produce, because they play no direct role in the decision making. When they have little real personal input or involvement in the job, performance means less to them.

These aspects of hierarchy all contribute to a lack of flexibility, which could be important to the survival of an organization faced with complex or ambiguous problems. In such situations the organization needs to have all members engaged in the correction of errors and the creative activity of problem solving. There are exceptions to this problem, as when hierarchies are comprised of subsystems that are interdependent and adaptive. But the development of such subsystems is atypical.[27]

Thus, the costs of hierarchy can be measured in terms of human potential: loss of worker satisfaction due to low status and lack of control over decision making; the costs to the administration of maintaining communication as well as surveillance and control of participants; and actual threats to the survival of the organization posed by a lack of flexibility or ability to adapt to complex and/or ambiguous situations.

So far, then, the concept of hierarchy has been examined from two perspectives: that of the rational systems theorists, who tend to emphasize the benefits of efficiency, security, and organization survival, and that of the natural and open systems theorists, who weigh these benefits against the economic and human costs. The "human costs" aspect of this critique has come primarily from the human relations school within the natural systems perspective. This school was responsible for bringing attention to the development of informal, more personal aspects of organization life and fostering the idea of *participatory management*. This approach aims to mediate some of the ill effects of hierarchy by sharing organizational information and decision making with those members or workers at lower levels. This school of thought is characterized by the work of Rensis Likert, whose leadership studies focused on ways in which lower levels of management could relate to higher levels within the hierarchy.[28] Chris Argyris's work focused on methods of reducing alienation by increasing the scope of certain jobs or rotating them.[29] In a similar light, Douglas McGregor's work centered on the restrictive nature of hierarchy with regard to worker input and satisfaction.[30]

While the idea of participatory management has been around for decades, it is currently receiving renewed attention. For instance, Du Pont has for some time now been stepping up its attempts toward worker participation through the "quality circle" or "team approach." As one Du Pont executive explains:

> The premise is simple—the level of thinking and the ultimate performance of supervisor and supervised can be significantly and permanently improved through communication and joint participation in problem solving.[31]

For Du Pont this has meant an increase in productivity, as well as improvements in manufacturing, marketing, and distribution of products. In addition, the company claims to have been able to reduce the need for direct supervisors due to increased employee participation. They reduced from seven to four the number of supervisory levels in several of their plants. Thus, the company has reduced the cost of its administrative overhead while at the same time increasing productivity. Currently, General Motors is implementing a similar plan.

While there are clearly benefits to such an arrangement, it is important to note that these must still be measured in terms of organization efficiency. While Du Pont was able to reduce a few levels of administration, the overall hierarchy itself was not altered significantly. Thus, the natural systems critique of hierarchy is limited in that it still works within the same boundaries put forth by the rational systems perspective. This problem has led to the following critical perspective critique of human relations:

> The history of organization theory may be seen, in part, as a process in which a series of 'nonrational factors' have been conjured up only to be subdued by the rationalizing core. Thus in the 1930s human relations theory arose as a champion of the informal structure. The trust of human relations theory, however, was to harness and control the informal in the interest of rationality.[32]

Thus, from a natural systems perspective, hierarchy, as a system of domination with efficiency as a primary goal, is still endorsed. This is also true of the open systems perspective, which is concerned with organization adaptation, "fit," and ultimate survival within its environment. While this perspective acknowledges that hierarchy is not appropriate for every organizational circumstance, it still reflects the dominant dictum of inevitability with regard to hierarchy. Nonetheless, the open systems approach does provide a theoretical bridge to the critical perspective of organizations, by recognizing the role of the environment in determining organization structure or reinforcing hierarchy, and that a kind of "natural selection" enables the survival of those organizations that "fit" with the environment.

The critical perspective operates on a much broader level than the natural and open systems perspectives, however. As explained earlier, this perspective considers how the dominant values in society foster or support broad patterns of organization structure, such as hierarchy. Thus, the critical perspective is as much an examination of dominant values in society as of the prevailing organizational structures. A first step in the development of this perspective was Victor Thompson's work *Modern Organization,* in which he argues that hierarchy is culturally determined.[33] Because hierarchy is treated as the only way to "organize," he states, those organizations that do not reflect this structure are considered to be "unorganized," even unworthy of the label "organization." Here Thompson has identified a dominant perspective in operation, one that allows for only hierarchical arrangements.

At the center of the critical perspective critique of hierarchy is the question of social control. The argument is that goal efficiency in organizations is only half the picture. The more pressing problem is that of those in power who wish to maintain their position without threat

from those at lower levels. This theory draws on recent Marxist schol-
arship on the historical evolution of the labor process in the United
States and Western Europe.[34] Fear of the development of trade unions
and worker uprisings gave managers an incentive to seek out more
effective means of control over workers. Hierarchy and the development of bureaucracy provided the means.

> Detailed division of labor and associated bureaucratic mechanisms
> encouraged workers to internalize the values and structures of the
> industrial workplace. To the degree that this occurred, employers
> were successful in creating a climate of greater social control . . .
> capitalism has developed a production process which not only de-
> livers the goods, but also controls its workers.[35]

From this discussion it is clear that theorists within the critical perspective would define and criticize hierarchy as a system of domination flowing from capitalistic values. They would argue that there is
a difference between efforts at efficiency and efforts at efficiency of
control, and that hierarchy is more useful for the latter than the former. In fact, they would argue that in terms of efficiency of production, hierarchy fails.

This perspective builds on criticisms of hierarchy already discussed
with regard to worker alienation, which suggest that productivity would
be dramatically increased if workers were not cut off from decision
making, control over their own jobs, and information about the organization. Given their low status and lack of meaningful rewards,
workers would rebel against the system were control not exerted from
the top of the organization and the larger society. If the prevailing
societal values did not reinforce hierarchy, this control would not be
possible.

> Fundamentally, internal structure is only capable of taking strategic
> advantage of coercive market forces that already exist. Without a
> labor market that would make disobeying orders costly, adminis-
> trative procedures would probably not be very effective in main-
> taining control.[36]

The most important aspect of the critical perspective is that it does
not take hierarchy to be inevitable. Rather than supporting this dominant view, the critical perspective puts forth a dialectical analysis that
"takes the rationalized organization as an arbitrary model unevenly
imposed upon events and insecure in its hold."[37] This analysis allows
us to examine the societally reinforced, market-related values that determine hierarchy and to consider how changes in those values could

lead to other organizational forms. Thus, the critical view places the development of hierarchy in a historical/cultural perspective that allows for consideration of new structural possibilities.

NOTES

1. Larry D. Spence, "Prolegomena to a Communications Theory of Human Organizations" (unpublished manuscript, Department of Political Science, University of California, Berkeley, January 1969), p. 12.
2. Roger Scruton, *A Dictionary of Political Thought* (New York: Harper & Row, 1982), p. 202.
3. Ibid.
4. Ibid.
5. Ibid.
6. Ibid.
7. Richard W. Scott, *Organizations* (Englewood Cliffs, N.J.: Prentice-Hall, 1981), p. 65.
8. Ibid.
9. Philip Selznick, *Leadership in Administration* (New York: Harper & Row, 1957).
10. Scott, p. 147.
11. Spence, p. 15.
12. Peter Blau and W. Richard Scott, *Formal Organizations* (San Francisco: Chandler, 1962), pp. 116–28.
13. Ibid.
14. Spence, p. 15.
15. Scott, p. 60.
16. Ibid., p. 63.
17. Ibid., p. 61.
18. Ibid., p. 149.
19. Theodore J. Lowi, *The Politics of Disorder* (New York: Basic Books, 1971), p. 78.
20. Selznick, p. 113.
21. Ibid., p. 56.
22. Ibid., pp. 56–64.
23. Herbert Kaufman, *The Forest Ranger* (Baltimore: Johns Hopkins University Press, 1967), pp. 210–13.
24. Daniel J. Elazar, *American Federalism: A View From the States* (New York: Crowell, 1972).
25. Scott, p. 149.
26. Ibid., p. 150.
27. Ibid.
28. Rensis Likert, *New Patterns of Management* (New York: McGraw-Hill, 1961).
29. Chris Argyris, *Personality and Organization* (New York: Harper & Row, 1957).
30. Douglas McGregor, *The Human Side of Enterprise* (New York: McGraw-Hill, 1960).
31. H. Gordon Smith, "A More Open Workplace," *Nations Business* May 1986, p. 6.

32. J. Kenneth Benson, "Organizations: A Dialectical View," in Mary Zey-Ferrell and Michael Aiken, ed, *Complex Organizations: Critical Perspectives* (Glenview, Ill.: Scott, Foresman, and Company, 1981), p. 270.

33. Victor A. Thompson, *Modern Organization* (New York: Knopf, 1961).

34. Paul Goldman and Donald R. Van Houten, "Bureaucracy and Domination: Managerial Strategy in Turn-of-the-Century American Industry," in Zey-Ferrell and Aiken, p. 192.

35. Ibid., p. 193.

36. Kenneth McNeil, "Understanding Organizational Power: Building on the Weberian Legacy," in Zey-Ferrell and Aiken, p. 51.

37. J. Kenneth Benson, "Organizations: A Dialectical View," in Zey-Ferrell and Aiken, p. 270.

THREE

Non-Hierarchy

As indicated in the first two chapters, organizations stemming from the critical perspective have received less attention within the literature than those flowing from the dominant perspective. Attempting to operate in the absence of hierarchy, rather than simply by reducing hierarchy, these organizations have deviated from mainstream notions of structure.[1] They operate primarily through a consensual decision-making process, which means that after an issue has been discussed by organization members, "one or more members of the assembly sum up prevailing sentiment, and if no objections are voiced, this becomes agreed-on policy."[2] While this type of organization has been referred to as collectivist or cooperative, the term *consensual* will be used to describe it here. Thus, *consensual organization* can be defined as "any enterprise in which control rests ultimately and overwhelmingly with the member-employees-owners, regardless of the particular legal framework through which this is achieved."[3]

Among the most recent comprehensive research with regard to consensual organization is that of the sociologists Joyce Rothschild and J. Allen Whitt. Their study of five different consensual organizations has produced a model that contains the following elements: authority, rules, social control, social relations, recruitment and advancement, incentive structure, social stratification, and differentiation.[4] The following discussion provides a summary of their work, as well as a comparison of the features of consensual structure to their counterparts within hierarchical/bureaucratic structures.

1. *Authority:* In contrast to the ideal bureaucratic structure, in which
   authority is vested in the individual according to position or rank
   within the organization, authority in the consensual organization
   rests with the collectivity. If authority is delegated by the whole,
   this is done temporarily and is subject to recall by the group.
   "Compliance is to the consensus of the collective, which is always
   fluid and open to negotiation."[5] In the bureaucratic structure,
   "compliance is to universal fixed rules as these are implemented
   by office incumbents."[6]
2. *Rules:* In the consensual organization, rules are minimal and based
   on the "substantive ethics" of the situation. In the traditional organization, rules are fixed, and emphasis is placed on conformity
   to the rules.
3. *Social control:* For the consensual organization, social control is
   based on something akin to peer pressure. Social control rarely
   becomes problematic, because of the homogeneity of the group.
   Such homogeneity is usually a conscious aspect of membership
   selection. Within a bureaucracy, social control is achieved through
   hierarchy and supervision of subordinates by their superiors, according to the formal and informal sanctions of the organizations.
4. *Social relations:* For the collective, social relations stem from the
   community ideal. "Relations are to be holistic, personal, of
   value in themselves."[7] In the traditional model, the emphasis is
   placed on impersonality, which is linked to a sense of professionalism. "Relations are to be role based, segmental, and in-
   strumental."[8]
5. *Recruitment and advancement:* In the consensual organization, recruitment is based on friendship networks, "informally assessed
   knowledge and skills," and compatibility with organization values.[9] The concept of advancement is generally not valued, since
   there is no hierarchy of positions and related rewards. Within
   the bureaucratic model, recruitment is based on formal qualifications and specialized training. The concept of advancement is
   very meaningful for an individual's career and is based on formal assessment of performance according to prescribed rules and
   paths of promotion.
6. *Incentive structure:* For the consensual organization, "normative
   and solidarity incentives are primary; material incentives are secondary."[10] For bureaucracy, "remunerative incentives are primary."[11]
7. *Social stratification:* The consensual organization strives to be
   egalitarian. Any type of stratification is carefully created and
   monitored by the collectivity. In the bureaucracy, there are "dif-

ferential rewards" of prestige, privilege, or inequality, each justified by hierarchy.

8. *Differentiation:* In the consensual structure, division of labor is minimized, particularly with regard to intellectual versus manual work. Jobs and functions are generalized, with the goal of "demystification of expertise."[12] Bureaucracy maximizes division of labor to the extent that there is a "dichotomy between intellectual work and manual work and between administrative tasks and performance tasks."[13] Technical expertise is highly valued and specialization of jobs is maximized.

The typology above represents an ideal type in both the consensual and bureaucratic cases. No one organization is likely to fit all or even most of the components of either type. Yet each ideal defines one end of a continuum of organization structure along which organizations will fall. The contribution of the Rothschild and Whitt typology is that it defines the organization structure that flows from the critical perspective of organizations. A foundation is gained from which to study the kinds of organizations that have until now been largely ignored. Within their study, Rothschild and Whitt also indicate those factors which they believe limit the ability of an organization to achieve a non-hierarchical structure. The following is a summary of those factors:

1. *Time:* Rothschild and Whitt indicate that consensus-style decision making takes more time than bureaucratic decision making, in which an administrator simply hands down a decision according to prescribed procedures. The idea of consensus, in which every member of an organization must agree to a decision, conjures up the picture of long, drawn-out sessions in which members may never agree. However, real-world experience has demonstrated that the endless rules and regulations of bureaucracies can also lead to protracted disputes. By contrast, in a homogeneous consensual organization, the consensual process can move very swiftly. The issue of time is specific to the issues and circumstances facing the organization. It is important to recognize that both bureaucracies and consensual organizations are capable of making decisions quickly or slowly, depending on the nature of the issue.

2. *Emotional intensity:* The study by Rothschild and Whitt indicates that there is more emotional intensity in the consensual setting. Consensual organizations provide face-to-face communication and consideration of the total needs of the individual. As a result, conflict within the organization may exact a much higher per-

sonal cost; individuals are held more accountable for their actions. In the bureaucratic organization, impersonality and for-
mality make conflict less personal and therefore easier to handle.
But bureaucratic procedure also alienates people and is less sat-
isfying personally. As in the case of time constraints, degree of
emotional intensity has positive and negative aspects for members of both organization types.

3. *Non-democratic habits and values:* Rothschild and Whitt point out
that as members of a hierarchical society, most of us are not well
prepared to participate in consensual styles of organization. Our
earliest contact with organizational life in educational and other
settings is bureaucratic. The earliest opportunity for learning
egalitarian values is in the home. Anarchist feminists have stressed
that patterns of domination learned within the family are likely
to be repeated within other organizations. Learning values that
support egalitarian behavior may predispose one to egalitarian
structures later in life.

4. *Environmental constraints:* While all organizations have some environmental constraints—economic, political, or social pressures
from the outside—Rothschild and Whitt argue that such constraints are more intense for consensual organizations because
such groups often form around issues that run counter to the
mainstream of society. While this point is well taken, consensual
organizations can also at times benefit because they provide a
service or offer an avenue of participation that is not available
through other organizations. This has been true, for example,
of organizations providing alternative health care or food co-ops
providing natural or organically grown foods.

5. *Individual differences:* This fifth and final constraint pointed out
by Rothschild and Whitt centers on the individual within the organization. They argue that while bureaucracies are able to cap-
italize on differences in the attitudes, skills, and personalities of
individual members, such differences may pose a problem for
organizations based on consensual process. For consensual organizations such diversity may lead to conflict. Yet while this point
has merit, it paints a somewhat false picture of both bureaucratic
and consensual organization. Students of bureaucracy are well
aware of the arguments regarding the question of diversity within
such organizations. Some argue that bureaucracy breeds same-
ness, encourages lack of creativity, and provides little in the way
of reward for anyone attempting to break out of set patterns.
When such rewards do exist, they are reserved primarily for those
at the top of the organization. Yet others have pointed out that
bureaucracies, or at least public bureaucracies, have the most di-

verse membership of any institutions. Thus, it is unsurprising that members of consensual organizations, which are frequently homogeneous, are likely to agree on issues that face the organization.

The various constraints indicated by Rothschild and Whitt in their study and development of the consensual model raise interesting and important questions. However, it is also important to recognize that the abovementioned points apply to all forms of organization in one way or another. The picture of consensual versus bureaucratic organization is not as black and white as recent research has implied. Myths regarding the good and bad points of each type abound. As research on consensual organization develops, it may serve to dispel these myths in a way that allows for clearer consideration of the possible usefulness of each model.

EXPERIMENTATION WITH CONSENSUAL STRUCTURE

The importance of studying consensual structure has been underscored by students of organization behavior, such as Ouchi, who are interested in shared values as a mechanism of control in high-technology industries.[14] While studies of these systems have contributed to an understanding of consensual structure, they hardly represent a body of literature considered essential to the study of organizations.[15]

Nonetheless, in the United States there is historical evidence of the existence of more than 700 consensual organizations from 1790 to 1940.[16] The development of co-ops followed major movements for social change in the 1840s, 1860s, 1880s and 1920s to 1930s. A fifth, and perhaps the most important period of development has occurred since 1970, in the aftermath of social change in the 1960s. As of 1976 there were 5,000 consensual organizations in the United States, with an estimated 1,000 new organizations added each year.[17]

Given this growth of consensual-style organizations, it is important to focus on what has been learned, and what can be learned, about their structure and operation. What follows is in no way a comprehensive review of the literature on non-hierarchy or consensual organization. Such a review is beyond the scope of this study. What does follow is a brief summary of the outcomes of research on some of the better known experiments with such structures.

First, such studies show that the primary goal of these organizations is *de-alienation*. The goal is to humanize the workplace, to put meaning and values back into jobs in order to reconnect the worker with society. Second, studies show that the ability to attain this goal is a function of the level of commitment to the goal on the part of the workers. Economic gain is also a factor; where monetary concerns are highest, the ability to achieve the goal of de-alienation is lowest. Third, the means for achieving this goal is reduction of hierarchy, as it is believed that hierarchy leads to task specialization and division of labor, which increases alienation. This research very clearly reflects the critical perspective, in its focus on the relationship of societal values to organization structure.

Of the well-known studies on consensual organization, most have focused on three major systems: Israeli kibbutz organizations, Yugoslavian worker organizations, and the somewhat lesser-known Mondragon group in Spain. Of these, the kibbutz is perhaps best known. It has been described as a small, rural, "total" community in which "work life, family life, and social life are closely integrated."[18] Its main goal is to completely enmesh the individual within the society.

In order to achieve this, decision making is shared and an egalitarian system is strived for in every aspect of the organization. "Decision making is generally face to face, leadership positions elected and rotated, and hierarchy is actively discouraged."[19] The entire organization meets once a week in a general assembly and an intricate committee system operates as well. It is important to recognize that the system of rewards is linked to the collective, not the individual. In this type of organization it is not desirable, from a personal standpoint, to hold a leadership position, for there is no internal hierarchy of rewards connected to position. The highest reward is simply membership in the collectivity.

The second best-known consensual-style organization is the worker-managed system in Yugoslavia. It represents the only nationwide system of its kind in the world. Each work enterprise is viewed as "social property" temporarily governed by the workers.[20] "By law, overall policy in every enterprise with more than ten workers must be formulated by worker's council, which elects (and may remove) the management board and plant director."[21] The worker council sets the overall "critical" policy, while the director and the board run the operation on a day-to-day basis. It is the goal of the Yugoslav leaders to have every enterprise in the country worker-managed.

A third cooperative is the Mondragon group in Spain. This is a group of over 85 manufacturing cooperatives with more than 18,000 worker members, representing one of the most vital aspects of the Spanish economy. Each member shares in the group's surplus "on the basis of wage rate and total hours worked."[22] Formal authority in each co-op is drawn from a general assembly which meets once a year and elects a board of directors. They also elect top managers who appoint managers at lower levels. The organization is aligned with a cooperative bank that provides the necessary financial services and support. "Mondragon is organized on the principles of shared ownership, egalitarianism (a maximum three-to-one spread on wages and salaries), and democratic control on a one-person, one-vote basis."[23]

These three organizations represent attempts toward non-hierarchy in the workplace. Their major goal has been one of de-alienation, of humanizing work and allowing workers to become reconnected to society. According to Greenberg's analysis, both the Yugoslav and Mondragon systems have failed in this respect because the workers do not have control over technical production. Instead, production has been organized according to scientific management principles. There is thus an extreme disparity between control over general policy and control over the specifics of implementation. As Greenberg explains:

> Formal ownership by workers does not necessarily mean worker's control of production. . . . The result, in addition to the exercise of control from the top, has been as extreme division of labor, mechanized, assembly-line operations with little regard for human needs, and extensive routinization.[24]

Greenberg's study of the plywood collectives in the pacific northwestern United States provides additional evidence of the difficulties of minimizing hierarchy with regard to technical production.

The kibbutz has come closest to decreasing alienation. It is argued that this is because of the overriding commitment to the political ideals of "liberated labor."

> Liberation means overcoming all forms of alienation which modern society inflicts on working man through technological systems of work, bureaucratic organization, and the status of one who must sell his labour.[25]

This is accomplished through job rotation and the selection of technical processes that maximize human potential. Small-scale division of labor has not been eliminated, but it has been significantly reduced.

It is important to consider the differences in goals among these three systems. For both the Yugoslav and the Mondragon systems, economic incentives and rewards form an integral part of the organization. For the kibbutz, social and collective goals are far more important. While all three organizations strive for the reduction of alienation in the modern industrial world, the kibbutz is clearly the most committed, and its members reflect this view. It appears that there is a relationship between ideology and the structure of organizations. One might speculate, with regard to the other two organizations, that ideology is not strong enough to override the constraints placed on the organization by the prevailing economic system.

NOTES

1. It should be made clear that non-hierarchical organizations have structure. This point will be addressed again in Part II.

2. Jane J. Mansbridge, *Beyond Adversary Democracy* (New York: Basic Books, 1980). p. 32.

3. Joyce Rothschild and J. Allen Whitt, *The Cooperative Workplace* (Cambridge: Cambridge University Press, 1986), p. 2.

4. Ibid., p. 62.

5. Ibid.

6. Ibid.

7. Ibid.

8. Ibid.

9. Ibid.

10. Ibid.

11. Ibid.

12. Ibid., p. 63.

13. Ibid.

14. William Ouchi and Jerry Johnson, "Types of Organizational Control and Their Relationship to Emotional Well-Being," *Administrative Science Quarterly*, 23 (June 1978). pp. 293–317 Also see research on the Japanese theory of the firm.

15. Rothschild and Whitt, pp. 1–24.

16. Ibid., p. 10.

17. Ibid.

18. Edward S. Greenberg, *Workplace Democracy* (Ithaca, N.Y.: Cornell University Press, 1986), p. 100.

19. Ibid.

20. Ibid., p. 101.

21. Ibid.

22. Ibid., p. 100.

23. Ibid.

24. Ibid., p. 108.

25. Ibid., p. 109.

F O U R

The Starting Point of Feminist Theory

Like the critical perspective within organization theory, feminist theory views the development of hierarchy in a historical/cultural perspective that allows for consideration of new structural possibilities. In its assumption of the possibility for fundamental social change, feminist theory is supported by feminist practice: the experiences and work of women within the feminist movement.

ORIGINS OF AMERICAN FEMINIST ORGANIZATIONS

Origins of the American feminist movement can be traced to the nineteenth century and to the fight for women's suffrage that eventually led to women gaining the right to vote through the nineteenth amendment in 1920. This important achievement was the product of decades of hard work by women who were concerned with a range of issues affecting women's lives in the areas of education, work, family, legal rights, and reproductive freedom. Some of the earliest gains came in the area of education, as efforts to open some college doors to female scholars proved successful by the 1830s.[1]

The movement became politicized when women began working for the abolition of slavery during this same time.[2] Women grew aware that they were not accepted as equals by their male counterparts in the public/political sphere. They were prohibited from joining male abolitionist organizations and often prevented from delivering public speeches. Because of this exclusion, women began forming their own antislavery organizations, which soon became forums for discussion

35

of female slavery as well. In 1848 Lucretia Mott and Elizabeth Cady
Stanton called a Women's Rights Convention to be held at Seneca
Falls, New York, where 300 women and men together approved a
Declaration of Sentiments and twelve resolutions concerning women's
rights regarding the family, religion, property, and suffrage. Such
conventions were held annually in various locations until the beginning of the Civil War, at which time activities stopped. After the war
and the abolition of slavery, women resumed their own battle, attempting to get the word "sex" added to the proposed fifteenth
amendment aimed at prohibiting the denial of suffrage on account
of race.[3] Failing in this attempt, the women's movement began to focus more intensely on the issue of suffrage and grew to be identified
almost exclusively with that cause.

Two organizations formed around the suffrage issue. The National
Woman Suffrage Association was formed by Stanton and Susan B.
Anthony and, while making suffrage the key issue, refused to drop
other important issues of family, law, and religion. Lucy Stone and
others thus organized the American Woman Suffrage Association to
focus exclusively on the issue of suffrage in an attempt to seem less
radical than the other group.[4] But by the 1890s, the organizations
merged into the National American Woman Suffrage Association,
which focused entirely on the issue of obtaining the right to vote for
women. By that time, a third group had emerged that represented a
broader range of women's issues. This was the women's temperance
movement, which was working for laws to restrict the sale and con-
sumption of alcohol. Women in temperance organizations again had
found they were restricted from joining the male temperance groups.
They saw temperance as an issue primarily affecting women because
there were no laws protecting women against the violence and/or de-
sertion of alcoholic men.[5]

Although these groups continued their work, few gains toward suffrage were made until a militant suffragist, Alice Paul, formed a small
group known as the Congressional Union in 1913.[6] Through hunger
strikes, parades, and demonstrations, this group's activities mobilized
the movement sufficiently to exert enough pressure on Congress and
the states to bring about ratification of the nineteenth amendment on
August 26, 1920. So much energy had been devoted to this goal, however, that the women's movement "virtually collapsed from exhaus-
tion."[7] With the exception of a few organizations—mainly professional groups, such as the National Federation of Business and
Professional Women's Clubs (BPW) and "good government" groups

like the League of Women Voters—the movement would not be re-
vived again until the 1960s.

In 1961 President Kennedy created a national Commission on the
Status of Women that led to the formation of a citizen's advisory council
and similar commissions in all fifty states.[8] These commissions clearly
documented the second-class status of women in the United States,
yet the government did little to bring about change. This lack of action mobilized many who had been involved with the commissions to
join with Betty Friedan in founding the National Organization for
Women (NOW) in 1966.[9] Thus began one branch of the feminist
movement, later to be joined by organizations such as the National
Women's Political Caucus and the Women's Equity Action League as
well as the organizations like BPW that had existed since the 1920s.
The structure of all these organizations was top-down hierarchical,
with elected officers, boards of directors, by-laws, and other procedural rules.

A more grassroots branch of the movement began to form in the
late 1960s, comprised primarily of students and others who had worked
in the civil rights movement and had been forced into traditional
women's roles in the organizations there.[10] This branch of the feminist movement organized in small groups, called "consciousness-raising" or "rap" groups. Such gatherings intended to give women an
opportunity to discuss their experiences of sex discrimination, not only
defining its scope but also beginning to devise strategies for change.
The groups were committed to non-hierarchy and to experimenting
with organizational structure. They were not interested in formal
leadership and organization as it had developed in the larger groups
of the movement.

It has been said of these groups that they "accepted the ideology
of 'structurelessness' without recognizing the limitations of its uses."[11]
Certainly, many did come to recognize their limitations and from that
starting point began to experiment with non-hierarchical structure,
adopting the culture and principles of consensual decision making.
But many of the early consciousness-raising groups did have difficulty
with the unaccountable leadership that developed out of the media
attention accorded the burgeoning movement. Due to personal skills
and characteristics, some members were more sought after by the press
and became unofficial spokepersons for their groups. Because group
process had not placed them in these leadership positions, it could
not remove them either. This phenomenon has been referred to as
"the tyranny of structurelessness," in an attack on the undemocratic

nature of the very groups of the movement that were aimed at being the most democratic or participatory.[12]

Both branches of the movement served to mobilize women in the early 1970s to pressure Congress for an equal rights amendment (ERA). This was not the first time such an attempt had been made. In 1923 Alice Paul and the National Women's Party (previously the Congressional Union) had proposed a similar amendment. But the ERA they proposed would have made unconstitutional then-current legislation that protected women and children in the workplace by establishing maximum hour laws as well as minimum wage laws.[13] Because of this, social reformers such as Florence Kelley as well as powerful progressive unions opposed the amendment. While the ERA was introduced in every subsequent Congress for the next twenty years, opposition from progressive and union feminists, as well as other progressives and union rank and file, ensured its defeat every time.[14]

When the new ERA finally emerged from Congress in 1972, its major opposition came from the political right, "who saw the ERA, along with abortion, busing, and gay rights, as leading to the destruction of the family and the American way of life."[15] After a long struggle and ratification by thirty-five of the necessary thirty-eight states, as well as a three-year extension of the ratification deadline, the ERA failed to gain further support and died in 1982.[16] Similar amendments have since been proposed but have failed to gain congressional approval.

Since 1982, both branches of the movement have continued their work toward equality for women. The larger groups have continued to focus on legislative goals concerning issues of pay equity, reproductive freedom, child care, and electing more women to public office. Some of the smaller groups have not continued, while others have gone through interesting transformations in structure as they remain committed to non-hierarchy and grass-roots approaches to change. The goals and structure of these groups will be the subject of further discussion in Part II.

THE DEVELOPMENT OF FEMINIST THOUGHT

The starting point of feminist thought is intertwined with that of feminist practice. The theoretical path to Seneca Falls and the contemporary American feminist movement was paved by a number of works, beginning with Mary Wollstonecraft's *Vindication of the Rights of Woman* in 1792. Contemporary writers of that day, from Francis

Wright in the first part of the nineteenth century to John Stuart Mill in the middle to later nineteenth century, formed what we have come to identify as the roots of liberal feminist theory. In addition, the work of Sarah Grimké, Sojourner Truth, Elizabeth Cady Stanton, Susan B. Anthony, and Harriet Taylor argued for faith in rationality, a belief in education, a view of the individual as an independent being, and natural rights.[17]

These points continue to be articulated in the work of modern liberal feminists, who argue that "female subordination is rooted in a set of customary and legal constraints that block women's entrance and/or success in the so-called public world."[18] Liberal feminists claim that socially constructed differences between the sexes are the chief source of female oppression. "Gender justice, insist such theorists," requires us, first, to make the rules of the game fair and, second, to make certain that none of the runners in the race for society's goods and services is systematically disadvantaged."[19]

Liberal feminism is often associated with or defined as "women's rights feminism," aimed during the 1970s and 1980s at ratification of the ERA as well as the drafting and rewriting of other laws advocating pay equity, federally funded child care facilities, and reproductive freedom. Liberal feminists are interested in reducing or eliminating patriarchy from the larger institutions governing society.[20] Their strategies include demanding "opportunities that will allow (them) to achieve equality."[21] They argue that women must become involved in the current political process: "We will do it by getting into City Hall ourselves, or by getting into Congress ourselves."[22] Liberal feminists accept the reality of having to work within hierarchical organizations in order to work for equality.[23] It is this kind of political activity, practiced by the larger organizations of the feminist movement, that has become the hallmark of liberal feminist theory.

Feminist practice derived from Marxist and socialist feminist theory is less visible than that based on liberal feminist theory but nonetheless lends much to feminist discourse and to our understandings of systems of domination. Marxist feminists focus on the impact of capitalism on patriarchy, specifically the sharp division capitalism creates between public and private work. They argue that capitalism, as a system of power, dominates both men and women by forcing them into their respective traditional roles: men into the public sphere of paid labor and women into the private sphere of family and home. Therefore, male dominance over women can be traced to imperatives of capitalism: "It is only the separation of home from workplace, and the privatization of housework brought about by capitalism, that creates the appearance that women are working for men privately in the home."[24]

For Marxist feminists, elimination of capitalism means elimination of patriarchy. They are therefore interested in large-scale economic change.

> If all women—not just the relatively privileged or exceptional ones—are ever to be liberated, the capitalist system must be replaced by a socialist system in which the means of production belong to one and all. Because, under socialism, no one would be economically dependent on anyone else, women would be economically freed from men and therefore equal to them.[25]

Socialist feminists examine the interrelationship of capitalism and patriarchy, claiming that patriarchy can exist even in the absence of capitalism. They argue that by focusing only on women in relation to capital, Marxists give the issue of sexual relationships a secondary importance:"There is no such thing as 'pure capitalism' nor does 'pure democracy' exist, for they must of necessity coexist. . . . A society could undergo transition from capitalism to socialism and remain patriarchical."[26]

Socialist feminism may thus be the most integrative of all of the strands of feminist theory. It calls for the elimination of patriarchy in all spheres, both public and private, through a unified feminist perspective that recognizes the complexities of women's subordination.

Radical feminists reaffirm that patriarchy as well as capitalism oppresses women. They argue that not only the manifestations of male domination in the public sphere but those in the private sphere must be brought to light. "It is not just patriarchy's legal and political structures that must be overturned; its social and cultural institutions (especially the family, the church, and the academy) must also go."[27] Radical feminists maintain that gender roles are socially contructed and that male power rests at the root of that social construction. Radical feminists of the 1970s focused particularly on male power over female reproduction. They argued most directly against the antifeminist argument originally posed by Freud that "biology is destiny," calling for advances in technology that offer women reproductive freedom in such forms of as contraceptives, abortion, *in vitro* fertilization and artificial insemination. While radical feminism remains one of the most diverse of feminist perspectives, as Rosemarie Tong explains,

More than liberal or Marxist feminists, radical feminists have explicitly articulated the ways in which men have constructed female sexuality to serve not women's but men's needs, wants, and interests. What women must do, insist many radical feminists, is to reconceive female sexuality, this time in the image and likeness of women.[28]

This brief discussion of liberal, Marxist, socialist, and radical feminism highlights both the common ground and the differences in perspective among feminists. Yet a fifth group, postmodern feminists, have recently been interested in moving away from attempts, particularly those of socialist feminists, to create a universal feminist view. Postmodern feminists argue that the construction of absolute categories of feminist thought reflects patriarchal strategies in its determination to devise the one best way to characterize feminism.[29]

Postmodernism is useful in reminding us that no one strand of feminist theory illuminates the way. We can see what might be gained or lost by assuming one feminist perspective over another. However, it can be argued that this approach, in rejecting labels and categories, inhibits our ability to explore the relationship between feminist theory and practice. In order to understand how political and social change occurs, we need to be able to identify a context for feminist thought and action. As Nancy Hartsock argues:

> For those of us who want to understand the world systematically in order to change it, postmodern theories at their best give little guidance. . . . Those of us who are not part of the ruling race, class, or gender, not part of the minority which controls our world, need to know how it works. . . . At worst, postmodernist theories can recapitulate the effects of Enlightenment theories which deny the right to participate in defining the terms of interaction. Thus, I contend, in broad terms, that postmodernism represents a dangerous approach for any marginalized group to adopt.[30]

ANARCHIST FEMINISM

In keeping with the above argument, one category of feminist thought that is particularly useful to the study of organizations is anarchist feminism. Anarchist feminism derives primarily from the work of Emma Goldman, who emigrated to the United States from Russia in 1885 and published her feminist writings in *The Traffic in Women and Other Essays on Feminism*.[31] Like other anarchists of her day, Goldman argued for a society without government, without "man-made law," which she claimed rested on violence and coercion. She envisioned a society that would respect the individual and work toward social harmony.[32] It was a vision of life without domination and the hierarchical structures that support it.

Today's anarchist feminists tend to ascribe to the broader goals of radical feminism. But in the tradition of Emma Goldman, they remain keenly focused on hierarchy and questions of organizational structure.[33] As a result, their position remains unique within the various frameworks of feminist theory. In their focus on the development of structures that avoid the kind of coercive power transmitted through hierarchical organization, they offer particular arguments for organization theory. While questions of hierarchy and power are important to all feminist frameworks, none address it as specifically as anarchists.

As explained above, the broader categories of feminist thought focus on both material and non-material explanations of patriarchy.[34] They provide a vital analysis of the role of capitalism and social-psychological factors in fostering patriarchy. Anarchist feminism focuses more specifically on the public and private structures that enable these material and non-material systems of domination to work. Anarchist feminists examine the flow of power, as well as the nature of power, within hierarchical organization and seek to create alternative structures and power relations.

By alternative forms of organization, they mean groups in which leadership positions are rotated and responsibility is shared among group members. They thus attempt to "eradicate all the structural factors that create and maintain leaders and followers."[35] This is theory that must be practiced on a daily basis, they argue, and not put off in waiting for larger social change.

> For social anarchists . . . the revolution is a process, not a point in time; and how one lives one's daily life is very important. People don't learn that they can live without leadership elites by accepting socialist ones; they do not end power relationships by creating new ones.[36]

Instead, there must be a qualitative change in organization structures and a qualitative change in our notions of power.

POWER

As Rosabeth Kanter so aptly puts it, "Power is a loaded term."[37] For some, the definition has been a simple one: domination. Power is a situation in which "any actor A has the ability to get actor B to do something B would not otherwise do."[38] Or, as Hans Morgenthau states, "when we speak of power, we mean man's control over the minds and actions of other men."[39] The above definition of power has been widely utilized within the literature of political science in the twentieth century and, as indicated earlier, has formed a major part of the dominant theory of organizations. Power, defined as domination, supports hierarchical arrangements in organizations. As Kanter states:

> Because the hierarchical form of large organizations tends to concentrate and monopolize official decision making prerogatives and the majority of workers are subject to "commands" from those above, it would be natural to assume that any use of the term *power* must refer to this sort of scarce, finite resource behind hierarchical domination.[40]

However, there is another understanding of power that does not constitute domination, but rather the ability to accomplish goals. This definition of power as ability, energy, and strength has existed in the professional literature for at least as long as the previous definition linking it with domination. Berenice Carroll points out that the 1933 *Webster's International Dictionary* defined power along the lines of ability. The first meaning listed is "ability, whether physical, mental or moral, to act: the faculty of doing or performing something."[41] The second is: "Exerted ability to act or produce effect; exerted or active physical or mental strength; might; energy; vigor, force."[42] Not until a fourth meaning is listed does the word "control" enter the definition.

As Carroll points out, a host of definitions of power that do not imply domination also exist within the literature. For example, power has been defined as:

> Any activity where there is accomplishment, satisfaction of needs, mutual attainment of goals not distorted by unfortunate—that is, thwarting—experience. . . . To gain satisfaction and, particularly, security, is to have power in interpersonal relations.[43]

Another such definition explains power as "the expansive biological striving of the infant and states characterized by the feeling of ability, applying, in a very wide sense, to all kinds of human activity."[44] Still more definitions exist: Hobbes defines power as "man's present means to obtain some future apparent good," while Bertrand Russell calls it "the production of intended effects."[45] While feminist theory did not create this alternate understanding of power, it has served to bring it to light. The problem is how to apply these definitions of power within the literature as well as within the actual operation of organizations.

The difficulty, as Kanter points out, is that power defined as domination supports hierarchy, leading to a situation in which only the very few at the top of an organization have power while the rest of the members are limited in their ability to act or be effective. As she argues, "the total amount of power—and total system of effectiveness—is restricted, even though some people have a great deal of it."[46] When alternate understandings of power are engaged, people are able to maximize their abilities and get more accomplished. This does not restrict, but instead expands the resources available to organizations in terms of the capabilities and energies of the members. As Kanter states:

> The problems with absolute power, a total monopoly on power, lie in the fact that it renders everyone else powerless. On the other hand, empowering more people through generating more autonomy, more participation in decisions, and more access to resources increases the total capacity for effective action rather than increasing domination. The powerful are the ones who have access to tools for action.[47]

Within the feminist literature the discussion of these two different concepts of power has led to the development of the term *empowerment,* in reference to power as the ability to "do" or accomplish something.[48] This term has been criticized as one that sidesteps the main issue. The criticism raises a valid point in that power, as domination, must be directly challenged: considered on its own merits, or lack thereof. As Kate Millett states:

> An ideal politics might simply be conceived of as the arrangement of human life on agreeable and rational principles from whence the entire notion of power *over* others should be banished, but one must confess that this is not what constitutes the political as we know it, and it is to this that we must address ourselves.[49]

Yet "empowerment" is a concept that is becoming increasingly utilized and understood.

Empowerment becomes important in light of the earlier question regarding control in organizations. Power is associated with the notion of controlling others, while empowerment is associated with the notion of controlling oneself. Therefore, within organizations based on empowerment, members monitor themselves. In organizations based on power, there must be an administrative oversight function.

Evidence of this difference in self-control and administrative control has been provided through research on Japanese firms that operate on a consensual basis. As William Ouchi states: "In this condition (self-control), auditing of performance is unnecessary except for educational purposes, since no member will attempt to depart from organization goals."[50] Ouchi goes on to point out the importance of developing organizations that have this self-monitoring feature. He argues that in a post-industrial society, one in which highly technical industries require "uncertain and interdependent work," the costs of conventional oversight will be too high. Thus, the need for developing self-monitoring systems is ever increasing.[51]

The discussion raised by Ouchi's work demonstrates the broader implications and applications of the questions raised by feminists, particularly anarchist feminists, regarding power. At the very least the Japanese theory of the firm lends credibility to the argument made by feminists that there are other ways to understand power.[52]

THE CONVERGENCE OF FEMINIST THEORY AND ORGANIZATION THEORY

Like the critical perspective of organization theory, an anarchist feminist critique places the development of hierarchy in the historical perspective of the development of organizations. However, the historical perspective presented in the literature has been gender-blind. Analyses of the development of corporate structures have tended to focus on decision makers, those involved in setting the direction of the organization at the managerial level. Those persons working in support, service, or maintenance roles have generally been ignored, particularly in research derived from the rational systems model. Women, who tended to fill these support roles, were thus excluded from analysis. As Kanter indicates:

> Given the concentration of women in such maintenance-support functions as office work, it was likely that the position of women and other such workers, the demands of their roles, their particular structural situation, and their contribution to the system would be underexamined, as indeed these issues have been in the organizational literature.[53]

Organizations were being defined as "sex-neutral machines" as long as men and "masculine principles" were in control.[54] Yet Kanter ar-

gues that the sex composition of a group can have an impact on behavior with regard to power relations and hierarchy. She cites the
Hawthorne plant experiments of the 1920s and 1930s, which focused
on the role of small groups in worker productivity at Western Elec-
tric.[55] Those groups that appeared "co-operative and trusting" of
management were female; those "aggressive" and "suspicious" were
male. These differences in attitude played a significant role in the
internal dynamics of the organization. The aggressive and suspicious
behavior led to increased competition and emphasis on hierarchy. While
many aspects of the Hawthorne studies have been analyzed, Kanter
has been the first to consider the gender differences. Other well-known
studies in the organization literature have yielded similar results.

Until recently, aside from the work of Kanter, little had been done
within the organization literature with regard to gender and in particular the role of women in organizations. Within the last two decades, due to the work of Kanter, Carol Gilligan, Kathy Ferguson,
and most recently Hester Eisenstein, the feminist literature has begun
to address these questions.

Ferguson presents an important critique of modern bureaucracy
in her book *The Feminist Case Against Bureaucracy*. She defines bureaucracy as both a structure and a process. As a structure it is "a
fairly stable arrangement of roles and assignment of tasks."[56] As a
process she describes it as an "ordering of human action that evolves
out of certain historical conditions toward certain political ends."[57] She
stresses that bureaucracy be considered within the larger social context, thus taking a critical perspective of organizations. She describes
that context as one in which

> social relations between classes, races, and sexes are fundamentally
> unequal. Bureaucracy, as the "scientific organization of inequality,"
> serves as a filter for these other forms of domination, projecting
> them into an institutional arena that both rationalizes and maintains
> them.[58]

Ferguson's focus on bureaucracy is a broad one, viewing it as the
primary means of organizational functioning in the public world. She
makes the important distinction between public and private, indicat-
ing that women have been primarily relegated to subordinate positions in the private domain of the family and home. She advocates
an integration of the two worlds in a way that will allow the experiences of women to offer alternatives to bureaucracy.

In their role as subordinates, women's experience sheds considerable light on the nature of bureaucratic domination; in their role as caretakers, women's experience offers grounds for envisioning a nonbureaucratic collective life.[59]

In arguing that women do offer an alternative view of organizational life, Ferguson is quick to point out that this view is not based in theory so much as on the real-world experiences of women.

The feminist case against bureaucracy goes beyond the other critiques in that it constructs its alternative out of concrete and shared experiences of women, rather than out of a romantic vision of precapitalist life or an abstract ideal of "human nature."[60]

Ferguson's work has been vital in laying the groundwork for further study of women and organizations.

Most recently Hester Eisenstein has told the story of feminist interventions in the Australian bureaucracy.[61] Australian feminist bureaucrats, or "femocrats," as she calls them, have made policy gains in some areas, such as equal employment opportunity legislation, where American feminists have not. In a recognition that women must participate, at some point, in bureaucracies, Eisenstein asks questions about their experiences and the impact of women's interventions in large-scale organizations. As Eisenstein states:

There is still, to me, a fundamental issue that remains unresolved for feminists, and that is how we get from the values we hold dear— of collective, non-hierarchical, democratic behavior—to the outcome we seek, of a peaceful world safe for women and others now subject to discrimination, victimization, and oppression, without sacrificing these values in the rush to seize and use power on behalf of feminist ends.[62]

Having explored some of the more important questions raised by feminist interventions in organization theory, in the spirit of Eisenstein's inquiry, this book now turns its attention to feminist interventions in organization practice. These interventions have raised new questions about non-bureaucratic, non-hierarchical structures.

NOTES

1. Judith Hole and Ellen Levine, "The First Feminists," in (Jo Freeman, ed. *Women: A Feminist Perspective* (Palo Alto: Mayfield, 1979), p. 544.
2. Ibid.

3. Ibid., p. 551.
4. Ibid.
5. Ibid., p. 552.
6. Ibid., p. 554.
7. Ibid., pp. 554–56.
8. Jo Freeman, "The Women's Liberation Movement: Its Origins, Organizations, Activities, and Ideas," in Freeman, p. 558.
9. Ibid.
10. Ibid., p. 561.
11. Ibid., p. 556.
12. See Jo Freeman, "The Tyranny of Structurelessness," in Jane Jaquette, ed. *Women in Politics* (New York: Wiley, 1974).
13. Jane J. Mansbridge, *Why We Lost The ERA* (Chicago: University of Chicago Press, 1986), p. 8.
14. Ibid., p. 9.
15. Freeman, "The Women's Liberation Movements: Its Origins, Organizations, Activities, and Ideas." p. 564.
16. Mansbridge, p. 13.
17. See Josephine Donovan, *Feminist Theory* (New York: Ungar, 1986), pp. 1–30.
18. Rosemarie Tong, *Feminist Thought* (Boulder: Westview, 1989), p. 2.
19. Ibid.
20. Barbara Sinclair Deckard, *The Women's Movement* (New York: Harper & Row, 1979), p. 445.
21. Zillah R. Eisenstein, *The Radical Future of Liberal Feminism* (New York: Longman, 1981), p. 4.
22. Ibid., p. 179.
23. This is not an endorsement of hierarchy on the part of liberal feminists. It is simply a recognition of the structure of the real world of politics.
24. Lydia Sargent, *Women and Revolution* (Boston: South End, 1981), p. 5.
25. Tong, p. 2.
26. Sargent, p. 17.
27. Tong, p. 3.
28. Ibid., p. 72.
29. Ibid., p. 17.
30. Nancy Hartsock, "Foucault on Power: A Theory for Women?" in Linda J. Nicholson, ed. *Feminism/Postmodernism* (New York: Routledge, 1990), p. 160.
31. Nancy Love, *Dogmas and Dreams* (Chatham, N.J.: Chatham House, 1991), p. 349.
32. Ibid., pp. 343–44.
33. See H.J. Ehrlich, Carol Ehrlich, David DeLeon, and Glenda Morris, *Reinventing Anarchy: What Are Anarchists Thinking These Days?* (London: Routeledge and Kegan Paul, 1979).
34. See Tong, pp. 1–9.
35. Sargent, p. 116.
36. Ibid., p. 114.
37. Rosabeth Moss Kanter, *Men and Women of the Corporation* (New York: Basic Books, 1977), p. 260.

38. Robert A. Dahl, "The Concept of Power," *Behavioral Science* 2 (1957), pp. 201–18.

39. Berenice A. Carroll, *Peace Research: The Cult of Power* (paper read at the annual convention of the American Sociological Association, Denver, Colorado, September 1, 1971), p. 586.

40. Kanter, p. 260.

41. Carroll, p. 588.

42. Ibid.

43. Ibid.

44. Ibid.

45. Ibid.

46. Kanter, p. 260.

47. Ibid.

48. See Nancy Hartsock, *Money, Sex and Power* (Boston: Northeastern University Press, 1985), pp. 224–26.

49. Kate Millett, *Sexual Politics* (New York: Doubleday, 1970), pp. 23–24.

50. William Ouchi, "Markets, Bureaucracies and Clans," *Administrative Science Quarterly* 25 (March 1980): 138.

51. Ibid.

52. See William Ouchi and Alfred M. Jaeger, "Type Z Organization: Stability in the Midst of Mobility," *Academy of Management Review* 3 (April 1978), 305–14.

53. Kanter, p. 405.

54. Ibid.

55. See W. Richard Scott, *Organizations,* (Englewood Cliffs, N.J.: Prentice Hall, 1981) p. 86, for brief description of the Hawthorne experiments.

56. Kathy E. Ferguson, *The Feminist Case Against Bureaucracy* (Philadelphia: Temple University Press, 1984) p. 6

57. Ibid.

58. Ibid., p. 8.

59. Ibid., p. 26.

60. Ibid., p. 27.

61. See Hester Eisenstein, *Gender Shock* (Boston: Beacon, 1991).

62. Ibid., p. 3.

PART TWO

F I V E

The Feminist Peace Group

The idea to start a feminist peace group resulted from a meeting of the women's caucus of the area peace coalition. Women from the coalition talked with other women who had formed similar peace groups in other communities. There seemed to be enthusiasm for the concept; those interested signed a list and were later contacted to attend an organizational meeting. At that meeting it was decided that the group would be all-female, feminist in orientation, and would affiliate with a larger international organization that had much earlier formed around the goals of peace and justice. This organization had formed in 1919 following the second Women's Peace Congress in Zurich, Switzerland, and by the 1980s had branches all over the world, including in China, the Soviet Union and Eastern Europe.[1]

HISTORY

The local chapter organized immediately before the women's peace encampment held in Seneca Falls, New York, in 1983. Initially it drew membership in connection with that event. The group ran ads in the local newspaper and worked through the bulletins and newsletters of other local organizations and churches to inform community members of its establishment and desire for participants. Membership soon grew to a core group of 10 to 15 and a mailing list of over 100. Activities centered on supporting the Seneca Falls encampment, and the local group began selling flowers in the City Hall park to raise money for the encampment. Women from the local organization also attended the encampment. This early experience generated ideas for later activities, including a feminist orientation toward consensus decision making and the notion of organizing special work or project groups.

A reevaluation of the group's role and commitments occurred in 1984 following U.S. missile deployment in Europe. At that point the group decided to affiliate with the local Peace and Justice Center. This center helps to support a wide range of participating groups, as well as individuals interested in peace work and education.[2] It provides a speaker's bureau, library and reference room, bookstore with peace-related items, and office and meeting space for the affiliated groups. A paid administrative staff runs the center under the direction of the Peace and Justice board, which is comprised of representatives from each of the member groups. In addition to the peace group that is the subject of this study, the member groups include the American Friends Service Committee, Central America Solidarity Association, Companeras, the Inter-Religious Task Force on Central America, Parents and Teachers for Social Responsibility, Pax Christi, the Union of Concerned Students, the Committee for Irish Human Rights, the Nuclear Freeze Network, and the Women's Rape Crisis Center.

Following both the encampment and the missile deployment, the organization concluded that it needed to develop a structure to allow it to work toward its substantive goals and increase its size. The organization developed project groups to allow members to divide responsibility and also to encourage the involvement of new members. As a result, in 1984 two project groups formed: Redirection and Women for a Change.

Redirection is a media project with the following stated concerns: the threat posed by nuclear weapons and strategies and policies surrounding them; Third World intervention and self-determination; militarism; the environment; credible leaders and open government; and meaningful employment in a healthy domestic economy. The group aims to use creative media to articulate its message. It defines itself as "a production company for issue-oriented political media."[3] Money for media projects is secured through grants such as those issued by the Haymarket Group in Boston and other socially conscious New England corporations. The group has launched many successful projects, such as a poster show that has toured the United States. Members have also placed peace-related posters in the local airport and on the inside and outside of municipal buses. More recently, a series of radio ads has aimed at awareness of the negative affects of war toys.[4]

The second group, Women for a Change, has been less successful. Its primary goal has been to get the peace message out by targeting candidates for elective office who appeared to have particularly bad records on peace issues. The women working in this group distributed leaflets and other printed materials in the parking lots of local businesses, but thought the project had little local impact and were disheartened by the election of Ronald Reagan in 1984. Since then, a new project group has formed, called Community Action. This group will work against the production and sale of war toys through projects aimed at raising community awareness. The exact nature of these projects was unclear at the time of this study. The Women for a Change group has since disbanded.

OPERATING PROCEDURES

The peace group meets on the third Monday of every month in the Peace and Justice Center. Its project groups meet on the first Monday. At full group meetings, everyone sits in a circle in the center of the room. Someone volunteers to facilitate the meeting; she regulates discussion flow. (A different woman facilitates each time, until everyone has performed the task at least once.) The agenda is set at the beginning of each meeting, with two lists being formulated: one with announcements, the other, business. Before announcements, each person introduces herself in case new members or guests are attending. The facilitator ensures that everyone who wishes to speak on an issue does so, and when decisions need to be made, this is done by consensus. In other words, the group talks an issue out until it is clear that everyone agrees. In interviews, members indicated that there never had been an issue in the organization's history upon which consensus could not be reached.

When the women first take their places in the circle, there is some informal time to talk. During this period a facilitator emerges from the group. She will ask if anyone has announcements and will take down the names of people who want to make them. She asks for business items and lists those. This process is accomplished quickly, never taking up more than five or ten minutes. The meetings begin with each woman in the circle introducing herself and signing her name to a list, as a way of keeping an attendance record. The facilitator calls on people for announcements: then business issues are undertaken. Meetings average an hour and a half in length, including the social time at the beginning. The general atmosphere is relaxed, friendly, and non-threatening.

The stated mission of the organization reads as follows: the peace group "is a group of feminist activists working for disarmament and social justice in our community and the world." In addition, the group states that it:

> Embraces feminism as the most effective and comprehensive analysis of our political, economic, social, and military institutions. We see the rule of men over women as the model for other forms of dominance and oppression. And we strive for a radically different society which values cooperation, non-violence, nurturance and spiritual integrity.

> Places the priority on political action. We thus work in small groups which operate on consensus decision-making and shared leadership roles.

The group claims to rely on three kinds of members: active members who participate in project groups and retreats, supporting members who attend events and participate in telephone trees, and sponsoring members who provide financial support for ongoing projects and actions.

In addition to Monday night meetings of the full group and the project groups, the organization holds a fall dessert gala intended to attract interested new members. This buffet is donated and prepared by the members, held in the evening, and advertised in the local newspapers as a membership event with free child care provided. It is held at the Peace and Justice Center. The group gained three new members through this event in 1988. Another event, a spring dinner, is usually held at one of the local churches. It is intended to be a fund raiser. Tickets are sold in the community, and the peace group secures a guest speaker, usually someone of national prominence in the peace community. The group is responsible for preparation and service of the dinner. Revenues are earmarked for peace group projects.

A third annual event is a retreat designed to address organizational issues. The retreat in 1986 reorganized the two project groups, Redirection and Community Action, both focusing on war toys. It was also decided that all active, meeting-attending members would choose one or the other "event" on which to work, either the dessert gala or the dinner. Those events are seen as the real bread and butter of the organization, so it was considered important that everyone contribute to them.

The relationship of the local peace chapter to the international organization is at best loose. Each member of the local pays dues of $25, of which $10 goes to the national and international organization. Periodically, officers of the national organization will visit this group. Such visits and resulting correspondence are evidence of operating procedures of the group. The following statement was taken from a letter written to the local peace group by a national officer, after her visit to a meeting:

> As you know I have talked to a number of branches. The question of who will lead and the changing organizational patterns of branches was so evident that I wrote my July/August *Peace and Freedom* article on "Leadership and Support: How to Keep On Keeping On . . ." Branches seem to be going from more hierarchical, patriarchal structures to in some cases the exact opposite. What is needed is a middle of the road pattern whereby we can utilize the best of both methods.

> Speaking of problems to iron out, my problem vis à vis [your] branch is who is in charge—to whom do I write if I want something or need to communicate. On the Branch Leadership Form that came in September of 1985, [Jane] is listed as the Convener. I know that is different from Chair and I think I remember her saying at the meeting I attended that she is not the leader *or* convener. I may have misunderstood. . . .

> P.S. I just came across a sheet listing . . . members to be contacted for specific items and there after the word Convener (handles correspondence with the national organization) is [Jane's] name.

This statement by the visiting national representative shows frustration with attempting to identify a "leader" for the group. There is in fact no designated leader, either formally or informally.

An article written by this national representative about the way local groups were organizing also contained some interesting information. Excerpts include the following:

> Branches are struggling with what the role of leaders should be, how to structure branch work, and how to develop new leadership. Their leadership styles are evolving towards a more feminist, nontraditional, non-hierarchical style—a style that encourages members to share in leadership, decision-making and responsibility for branch work . . .

While some of our branches find themselves "on hold," others are charting innovative organizational paths. When no one wanted to chair . . . [one] branch, members formed a "gang of six," each with a specific task. The "gang" meets the week before a branch meeting to go over mail and choose an agenda and a chair. All decision-making is shared.

[Another branch] has no chair. Instead, one member facilitates meetings, another serves as treasurer, and others put out the news-letter. . . . [One member of yet another branch] notes that the ques-tion of leadership is a problem for the entire women's peace move-ment. She sees a growing reluctance among women to recreate patriarchal models in their organizations. Their branch now has a planning board of 24 members, each with a specific and manage-able task.

She says the peace group that is the subject of this research:

is a self-described group of feminist activists organized into project groups. This structure enables members to divide responsibility, share leadership and readily involve new members. The branch meets monthly, the project groups as often as needed.

She writes of another New England group:

The purpose of their organizing is not only to gain members for [the peace group], but to empower others to make the connections between our government's militaristic and racist policies and what's going on in their community. . . . The feminist style of leadership really works in their conservative rural area.

ANALYSIS

Data on this peace group were gathered through observation of approximately seven meetings, including one retreat and at least one committee meeting, over a two-year period. Membership attendance at meetings during the period of study was examined, revealing a core active group of approximately twelve members. Of these, eight were interviewed formally. One member of the supporting group who was once an active group member was also interviewed.

The formal interviews included a series of questions asked of all the women in all three organizations studied. During some interviews, however, additional questions grew naturally out of the discussion. Since the women in this organization are most directly focused on the issue of hierarchy, more probing questions were asked of them in some cases than of those in the other organizations. Of the three organizations, the women of the peace group tended to have the highest level of formal education, with at least three members holding doctoral degrees. It should be noted that many of these women, because of their education and careers, are more accustomed to data-gathering techniques than the other women and perhaps as a result are better able to articulate their views.

Operating Principles or Process

In the context of the peace group, the word *process* encompasses far more than specific procedures for decision making such as consensus or voting. Process for this group means an entire mode of behavior in and around the organization that is considered to be appropriate by organization members. In observing this group, one receives a sense of a relaxed, informal atmosphere. The Peace and Justice Center, where meetings are held, has the ambience of a comfortable library reading room or bookstore. Chairs and other furnishings are casually arranged and decorated in warm earth tones. People can often be seen sitting on the floor reading or quietly talking with a friend while working on some peace-related project. Walls are covered with shelves and displays housing peace paraphernalia from books and posters to T-shirts and jewelry. These items are for sale to the public, but the center does not have the hurried feeling of a store. It is a peaceful place.

During meetings, the member in a circle. By asking who would like to facilitate, they begin the process: defined by this group as a comfortable setting and an atmosphere of supportiveness, respect, and friendship. The appropriate behavior is relaxed, and reflects a commitment to mutual respect and concern for group members. The actual operating principles that comprise this process are those of consensus, empowerment, and emerging forms of leadership.

Consensus Consensus can be defined as participation by all members "in a collective formulation of problems and negotiation of decisions. All major policy issues . . . are decided by the collective as a whole. Only decisions that appear to carry the consensus of the group behind them, carry the weight or moral authority. Only these decisions, changing as they might with the ebb and flow of sentiments in the group, are taken as binding and legitimate."[5] For members of the peace group, then, consensus is a central operating procedure. As one member explains:

> I wouldn't have it any other way. It is absolutely what this peace group is. Nobody comes to a meeting assuming it will be another way. We don't even contemplate another way of being. There have been conflicts, but it is a function of talking until it is resolved. Sometimes we continue to talk until people compromise or change their minds or we decide a decision is not appropriate at this time. If that process were ever to change, I would have serious doubts about voting, which would have serious ramifications for everything they do.

At least three factors in the environment of this organization encourage members to feel consensus works well for them. The first is group homogeneity. While this group is fairly homogeneous in demographics such as age (mid-30s to 40s), level of education (high), and race (white), this is not what group members mean when they talk about homogeneity. They mean homogeneity of political outlook, commitment to peace and feminist issues—which to an extent is related to demographics.[6] Because they speak of operating from a common base, these women rarely disagree about the issues that concern them.

> We don't have to go into detail about our politics because there are a certain amount of experiences we've all had in common that people understand. It makes it comfortable. I think it would be harder without it [the common base]—time consuming. Process versus time is the issue in organizations. Some say consensus takes too long. If we had a great disparity in views in this group and only met once a month like we do, we would have a difficult time. I am not an adamant believer of consensus in all circumstances. I think it works well for us, but not for all organizations. Those [organizations] where people are coming from very different perspectives—it would take an enormous amount of effort and time and then they might never reach consensus.

As another member explains: "It is a comfortable group. What makes it comfortable is that members come to the group in points of their thinking or value systems and we don't have to sit around working all of that out. The group is already feminist and committed to feminist goals and consensus decision making."

Another important factor in operating by consensus appears to be the group size. The number of members attending meetings in the two-year period in which this organization was studied did not exceed fifteen. Small size seems to enhance this group's ability to function with consensus. One member explains it this way:

> I think as long as the group is as small as it is, it [consensus] works O.K. If you get a larger group where people don't know each other well, I think you'd have more of a problem. I think a lot of us think similarly, and that is an advantage. There are issues, if pressed, we would disagree on. I think what would separate us is if somebody came forward and said we've got to get out and do street theater or go climb the fence at G.E. There are things like that some of us can't do, I won't do. If that were demanded of us, we'd have a problem. We have had some disagreement on who should be allowed into the Peace and Justice Center. This was over the case of some groups that are not truly peace groups. But we get by that and come to common ground.

One advantage of small size is that people get to know each other better than they would otherwise, allowing them to find the common ground that makes consensus work. It may also be possible that an exclusionary function is at work, in that small size may make differences more apparent and eventually lead some members to leave the group rather than overcome those differences. At the time of study, however, there was no evidence to indicate that this process had ever occurred with regard to the membership of individuals in the peace group. Nonetheless, members speculate about the optimal group size for a consensual process. As one says, "Size can matter. I'm not sure if there is an optimal size." Organization theory literature is equally vague with regard to the size issue: "As organizations grow beyond a certain size they are likely to find purely consensual processes of decision making inadequate, and may turn to direct voting systems."[7] Questions about optimal size may hinge on a range of factors, including the goals and nature of an organization. While some members of the peace group are concerned about size, they have not yet reached a point at which they believe size has inhibited their ability to operate by consensus. One woman, however, offers this observation from another group to which she belongs:

> I've been involved in consensus decision making where there has been a hundred people and it is a pain in the neck at times. It is difficult and there are some people you want to strangle—it has been said, but they *have* to say it one more time. But I think that is part of the decision you make when you say everyone is entitled to be a part of a decision.

Another important factor contributing to consensus decision making, from the standpoint of organization members, is that they are women. Members of the peace group claim that women are better at consensus for several reasons. Chief among them are that women are better listeners, not accustomed to or interested in dominating meetings or shouting other people down in the course of discussions. One woman explains why she thinks women are better at consensus:

> It is a way that women have. In a women's group I think it is easier to speak out and to say what you think. There is more room. You see women exhibiting certain kinds of behavior, but in an all-women's group you usually don't have that type of thing in which people dominate the conversation and don't let other people speak and are attached to their own voice. When I started becoming politically involved I wasn't respected and wasn't listened to. And since then I have joined some of these groups again, but I am prepared for it and have learned to be better at speaking out. Also, I try to bring this awareness to mixed groups, that shouting people down isn't appropriate behavior.

Another member adds:

> I think there are very clear differences in women's groups and mixed groups. What a feminist group does with very little difficulty is what mixed groups try to do but never really succeed at. A lot of it has to do with the way women interact with each other and that women tend to be listeners.

On the issue of dominating meetings, one woman had the following to say about the difference between women's groups and a particular mixed-gender group:

> For example, take the Heart Association. The men dominate the meeting and not all of them are officers. They come from strong professions and they are not self-conscious about dominating. Often the women don't have confidence. One woman, who is president of the board with a very responsible nursing job, says things in a presentation like "I think" and "I guess." If I were at a meeting of the peace group and a woman made a presentation like that I would say to her, "That was a really great presentation, and you don't have to say, "I guess because you really knew that." I would be supportive, and you can't do that at [the Heart Association]. There is no bonding or helping women take their place. And then I think that's another whole difference—[of] what taking your place means. The assumption at the Heart Association and other groups like that

is that the norm is male-defined, and it is not male-defined at the peace group.

An operative belief here is that women's groups are more supportive of individual members and better at creating a non-threatening atmosphere in which consensus can be fostered. This includes showing consideration for people's personal lives, rather than professional identities, as part of what they bring with them to the organization. Consideration of personal lives has the effect of creating common ground, something everyone can relate to, whereas—in groups other than professional associations consideration of occupation can have just the opposite effect. That someone is a doctor or a lawyer can create inequalities in groups, especially if those individuals purposely make a point of their differences. Under such circumstances, it is difficult for group members to think they are on equal footing. They may feel intimidated by someone making an issue of his or her profession or work title, which could be a barrier to participation.

> Men carry over from their professional lives into these other settings. They care about their communities but it is also contacts for work; it is a form of marketing. When a CPA [certified public accountant] sits on the board and is the treasurer and everyone jokes about his being a CPA and his presentation—it is there. . . . When I go to the peace group there is time in the beginning where you catch up on how everyone is as a person. For these other groups, what you do professionally is important but what you do that isn't professional isn't important. Whether you have a family or whether it is a crisis—that isn't important. I think that is a coldness about these groups. Here you are working together in your free time. Some of what I do politically is also my social life, so I want to do it with people I like. It is not that women don't take themselves seriously; that's not the issue. There is a bigger picture of what life is and who they are.

Again, this statement emphasizes how important application of the concept of process is for this peace group. A foundation of friendship and supportiveness makes consensus easier. Members of the group claim that women are more likely to recognize the value of this more personal approach than men, and more likely to be skilled at it.

Avoiding domination by any one member or group of members within the organization is important. Members believe that consensus prevents domination, while voting can encourage it. Again, they emphasize that women are better at consensus and better at avoiding domination.

The idea of operating by consensus was considered to be part of a feminist framework, so that was the reason for having an all women's group. Too many of the peace organizations were not operating that way. There were a few people dominating them and personalities would get involved. So the whole issue around being a women's organization and consensus was all intermixed. . . . We came together because we share values and goals and we have a sense of respect for each other. When you are not talking in terms of voting, things don't become great issues. Our decision making is a continuing process.

Another member offers this perspective on voting:

When elections are close they tend to be very divisive. It is not necessary to talk things through and bad feelings are not resolved. At some point those feelings come home to roost. In the peace group, decisions don't tend to be made at all unless there is considerable consensus. Those who didn't initially agree don't feel left out and it gives them a healthy way to work toward something. If your view didn't carry one day, there is every reason to believe that it could another.

Yet another member feels that voting results from "the belief that you can't reach consensus. We believe that for anything that's important enough, consensus can be reached. If things are going to work well, the decision has to be made this way. Otherwise, there is coercion."

Yet organization members also feel some frustrations with consensus as a process. Three find it to be time-consuming:

Frustration always lies with the things that I feel are moving too slowly and again it is in the context of meeting once a month and I get impatient if we table something. But it used to happen more in the past. Now we are more task-oriented, and also some decisions take place in even smaller groups—the project groups. I think size is an issue. But satisfaction lies in the fact that every person ends up being committed to the decision we make and so when the decision gets made, people are much better able to live with it and there is satisfaction in knowing we all support it.

[Consensus] doesn't really mean that one or two people can block decision making. We sit and talk it out and come to an agreement on something that everyone can live with. The process matters; it is very important. It may take longer, but everyone is real conscious of that.

I think that in one way it is true [that consensus is not efficient], but efficiency may not be the best principle to apply to begin with.

The accusation of lack of efficiency tends to happen in contexts where the people involved aren't very committed to the principle of collective decision making.

While these women acknowledge that consensus takes time, the result is viewed as a win/win situation. Everyone can walk away from a decision feeling that she contributed to and can live with it. This is not generally true of voting.

Empowerment. In Part I of this research, power was defined as domination and identified as resulting in hierarchy in organizations. Empowerment, defined as energy or ability to accomplish mutual goals, is thought to be a major factor in development of non-hierarchical organizational structure. Data gathered from this peace group provide empirical evidence that a relationship can exist between empowerment and an absence of hierarchical structures.

Power as domination is clearly not something that members of the peace group find appropriate to their organization. Members do not like having to fight with other people in order to speak at meetings; they experienced too much of this in other organizations, in which men took leadership positions and dominated the group. As one member stated, "I wanted a group that would deal with peace issues, but didn't want to have to deal with the conflict and adversary relations that I find in most groups." Another added, "I don't need for that to happen in a volunteer organization that I belong to."

A major goal of this organization is to work toward world peace. In a global sense, they see power as domination leading to conflicts between nations, while empowerment can lead to peace. Thus, they feel, if organizations can be built upon the concept of empowerment, people will learn to stop dominating one another and eventually this will lead to peace in the world. This theory is stated explicitly in an organizational mission statement and characterizes this group as anarchist feminist rather than liberal feminist. This is why building and maintaining a non-hierarchical organization is so important to them. They admit there are problems, for those outside the group, in understanding the difference between power and empowerment. As one woman explains:

> Power is ominous. It is the power to deprive others of choice, of points of view, of seeing each other's value. Empowerment is those other things. It is a hard concept because it is so foreign to a dominance-based culture. It is not surprising that empowerment is a hard concept to define.

Another woman in the organization defines empowerment in this way:

> Empowerment is what you do for yourself. Power is what is bequeathed [to] you. Where you have an organization where people can take on different roles and you get practiced and skilled at doing new and different things, you have the potential for empowerment. In that situation where you have an organization where people become very strong in very specific roles, you have the risk of power-dominated situations. That rigidity of roles has a lot to do with the differences between the two.

Thus, empowerment is believed to be threatened by permanently placing individuals in certain roles. Others are then prevented from learning tasks and procedures surrounding different jobs. In this way, specialization becomes a form of hierarchy. By contrast, a rotation of roles increases the knowledge of all members, preventing specialization.

Emerging Forms of Leadership. The meaning of leadership in an organization like the peace group is different from that of hierarchically disposed organization. The notion of leadership in the peace group is not one in which power has been handed to someone. Instead, it emerges as a product of the capabilities and skills of individuals, in a way that is constructive to all members of the group. It involves rotation of tasks and a sense of collectivity, suggesting group rather than individual ownership of an outcome. Through this kind of leadership, individuals develop roles that only later grow to be defined by name. In a hierarchical setting, where roles are prescribed; here, roles are often "post-scribed," or written later, after individuals have developed them. As one member explained:

> People can be involved with any of the project groups they want to. They can participate and leave and do something else. There is no sense of one person being the expert on what all of the different project groups are about. That is where Redirection [the media project] had its greatest success. A lot of people contributed different talents to the process. For example, some people who are artistic can work on the visual things, others can pay attention to fundraising, and still others are better at the concepts. . . . When it comes to trading off specific tasks within project groups, we do that all the time. We rotate who is in charge of keeping track of finances, who is in charge of managing a particular grant . . . A good example is how we just branched out into radio and everyone was new to it. We are going to do a new radio project and now a member who

wasn't involved in it the first time is going to be involved—they are showing her how to do radio spots.

Another member explained leadership in this way:

I am a leadership-type person, a strong personality willing to speak up, and I have played that role. But the organization is real conscious of process. If I am facilitating the meetings too much, I make sure that others do it. The group allows me to do what I am good at and what I like, but without it infringing on others in the group. The group allows for this kind of relationship. It is built on respect and common values. Each member comes into the group with different skills and we utilize that without involving egos. Someone can work with me in what I'm doing and we can share leadership. Each person carries responsibility, so I monitor myself as does everyone. People become empowered to try things they wouldn't have tried and they grow this way.

Uniqueness of Structure

When asked who runs this organization, six of the nine members interviewed indicated that it was an inappropriate question:

The names that come to mind are the people who have been here the longest, but I wouldn't say that they run the organization at all. They are simply people I identify the organization with.

I think it is on equal footing. Some people have special talents. For instance, one member is good at leading a meeting and focusing on the real issues, getting us to the point. Another person is good at keeping records, keeping track of membership. Certain people play certain roles due to their skills.

I see people who focus and put a lot of energy in and that is different [from "running" the group]. We are more fragmented now into project groups, but our decisions are very conscious decisions, based on input of the whole group.

There are always people who have time to work more on this or that. Some people are more visible than others, but I don't think it is the same as having [permanent] leaders. But if certain people's ideas work and make the organization go, it is on those merits. It is not because somebody wields power, and somebody different can emerge at a different point. If the consensus is that a person's ideas have developed in a direction the organization doesn't want to go, there is no need to kick the person out. Those ideas simply cease to be persuasive.

Three members who answered the question in a more direct way indicated that the "active" group runs the organization in the sense that it makes policy.

> In a sense, policy is made by the people who come to meetings. But no one comes with the intent to "run" or dominate the process. Actually, the process wouldn't allow for it.

> The group is run by a set of women who meet once a month.

> When I was more active I would say there was a core of women who were the most active who were probably perceived as running [the organization], and that wasn't suppose to happen. There was a core of eight to ten who came regularly. Information is power. If you have more knowledge about what's going on, it is logical that you are going to be a part of the group leading. Others come in and out, but we have good ways of information sharing through various events.

From these statements and others, it is clear that the concept of leadership in this organization has led to the development of a structure in which active group members make policy. Other members support this group in ways that they choose, contributing money or volunteering with various projects. They emphasize a concept of leadership based on members' skills and interests. This concept has allowed also for development of project groups within the active group, and it has set a pattern for the organization's work. The following explanation from one member shows how this leadership concept helped to develop structure:

> We needed to figure out what we were going to do at the end of Seneca. We had a retreat and came up with two groups: Redirection and Women for a Change. . . . We evolved from there in a way that developed our work patterns. Everything gets done through project groups. In the beginning there was one woman who served as a real communication network for the organization. She would call people who couldn't attend meetings and tell them what went on, as well as call new members to explain to them how the organization worked and answer any other questions. When she moved out of this area we lost that function. Those things have to be done as a commitment to the group. What we have done now is divided into two committees: the dessert gala for fall and the dinner for spring. In the past the same people ended up doing both things. We have now restructured so that everyone is on one or the other of these committees.

Importantly, this organization's structure has emerged out of the skills members contribute. Interest in specific issues led to developing project groups through which certain tasks could be performed. One woman, due to her own interests and abilities, served as a communication facilitator. When she left, her role in the organization was not immediately taken up by or assigned to another individual. However, there was a recognition that what she had contributed was valuable. Over a period of years, the organization decided to restructure in such a way that everyone could participate in the communication function and recruitment of new members. Structural change came about by dividing organization members into dessert gala and spring dinner committees, allowing every member to participate in those functions.

The relationship of the active group to the supporting and sponsoring groups is an important issue. While the active group does make policy for the organization, it does not create a situation in which policy is passed downward and implemented by the other groups. Any member of any of the three major groups is able to participate in policy making by simply attending and participating in the monthly meetings. When policy decisions are made, they are communicated to other members who can then choose the ways in which they would like to participate, or they can choose not to participate at all. There is no top-down or vertical aspect to the organization; it might best be envisioned as three sets of intersecting circles. As one member has indicated, "I don't see any vertical to it. People can be involved with any of the project groups they want to. They can participate and leave and do something else." On the matter of participation, another member offers this explanation:

> If someone would have an idea and the group embraced that idea, but no one had the time or inclination to do it, the idea is dropped. If no one wants to do it, that's it. [Whereas] in other groups once an idea was determined to be a good one, then the group did a guilt trip on the people—that they should do this. The idea took precedent over the people, rather than the other way around. The content dominated and people did not have the freedom to say no, I don't want to do it. . . . What I liked was the sense that you had the freedom to participate on your own terms.

The issue of feeling pressured by the work or other members appears to be very important among members of this organization. As one explained:

We have groups working in different areas and we have a common theme, but in each group a person is given a part of the project and no one is calling you up to go and do things. It is your responsibility. . . . The other difference [between this group and mixed groups] is that we only take on what we can reasonably do. If we don't have someone willing to do it or the energy to take it on, we don't do it.

Another member explained the way the organization works in this way:

The women were active and very responsible. If someone said they would do something, it got done. It was also all right to say, "I can't do something," and not to have to feel guilty about it. And politically the analysis was very comfortable for me. It was really exciting to be around women thinking that way.

The sense of participation by supporting members reflects great ease in moving in and out of the organization, of participating on one's own terms. When asked why she is not an active member, one supporting member answered as follows:

It has nothing to do with the organization. I'm very active in the abortion rights league and the community health center. I have difficulty keeping other ongoing commitments. I, instead, would rather get involved in action. Tell me where to be and I'll be there, just don't ask me to plan it.

This statement reflects the way in which this member defines her participation as a supporting member. She could become an active member again or offer input into the active group at any time.

How the Organization Evolved

The fact that the peace group has evolved into the structure described above raises questions about differences between consensual and other types of non-hierarchial organizational structure. When the group was first formed, emphasis was placed on the decision making process, identified through discussion as consensus, empowerment, and leadership. Yet no particular structure was determined for getting work done in the organization. The group decided to work on and with the Seneca Falls peace encampment, as a group focused primarily on this event. At the end of the encampment the members began to consider what other issues they might wish to address. The project group structure developed at this time, with lists compiled of which members wanted to participate actively and which preferred to be only supporting members (providing money and attending events).

Since that time (1984), the media project group has continued, while the Women for a Change group has been replaced by a Community Action group. Additionally, there has been recognition of a communication function necessary for maintaining the organization, resulting in the increased participation of members in the two "event" projects, and in the annual retreat. As one member explained:

> We essentially had certain functions that have to happen in order for the organization to remain a viable and ongoing group. Those functions are membership recruitment, fund raising, and planning. We all need to take a role in all three, so membership recruitment now takes the form of the dessert gala, fund raising comes in the form of our yearly dinner, and planning comes through the retreat. What the group is about beyond that is that we've divided ourselves into two project groups. . . . We've also decided this year to focus on one theme for both project groups. The theme is war toys. . . . So what we have is all the members coming to meetings taking shared responsibility for these bread-and-butter issues of membership, etc., and then we have the task oriented groups.

In this way, the organization seems to have evolved from a consensual into a modified consensual structure. Refocusing the organization's goals resulted in this modification. The goals that have been adjusted are secondary, and not the primary goals of commitment to feminism, peace, and non-hierarchy.

Clarity of Goals. When asked to identify the organization's goals, members generally responded by saying they were working for peace and justice within a "feminist framework." They indicated that such a framework meant working through a consensual process and maintaining a non-hierarchical organization. If this large goal were to be compromised, all other goals would be too. This perception suggests clarity as well as ranking of goals, with process and structure of the organization representing the most important goal and projects focused on peace representing a secondary set of goals.

Members indicate that the clarity of goals helps to make consensus possible and keep factions from developing that might make reaching consensus more difficult. In factions, individuals begin to develop their own agendas and goals, which may not reflect those of the larger group. In interviews, members of this organization stressed their belief that goals, as well as outcomes, of the group's work were viewed as a product of the group rather than of individuals. One member explained as follows:

> What is interesting is that people like the affiliation of the organization but they don't define themselves by it. When we do things that are the peace group's things, there isn't one person's name associated with it. There really is a group ownership to what we do.

This commitment to group goals, and agreement as to what the goals are, are important aspects of the internal environment of the organization; they contribute to the organization's ability to operate by consensus.

Potential for Success. Members of the peace group indicate that their potential for success in creating and maintaining a non-hierarchical structure is greater because they are women, with experiences different from those of men. They feel that process as they define it is easier for women, because they believe women are better listeners and have more experience in working toward compromise. They also believe that women have greater respect than men for minority points of view and are better able to put personal agendas aside for the collective good. They indicate that their experiences in mixed gender groups have shown men frequently "take over." In such groups content counts more than process, meaning that completion of tasks often is more important than the way members are able to participate and interact with each other in the organization. They believe that, in general, the norm for group behavior in mixed organizations is male-defined.

Constraints. While the above discussion indicates that group members believe they have some advantages in developing non-hierarchical structure due to the internal environment of the organization, they have also experienced constraints in maintaining this type of structure. For this group, most of these constraints are internal. They are a volunteer organization and thus do not have to deal with the financial and economic constraints of a real business. They are under no particular time constraints to get work done, other than those which they create for themselves. They are not engaged in a dependent relationship with their national organization. While they have some affiliation with the national group, they pride themselves on being different from that group in developing their own operating procedures.

The group is dependent to some extent on external sources for money, such as grants provided by local and regional organizations. These grants fund major projects, such as the redirection media project, for which prime radio time has been purchased. The group is also dependent on the external climate with regard to membership recruitment. Membership in volunteer organizations has been in decline over the last few decades. This is due, at least in part, to the women's movement and the entrance of more and more women into the work force. In general, women have less time to devote to volunteer organizations and may be more selective as to the organizations in which they wish to participate.

The most significant constraint for the peace group is not unique to this organization. The constraint falls into the category of process versus task accomplishment. Several members of the organization indicate a concern over the fact that as the organization has evolved, less time has been spent on process and more time spent dealing with the actual business of the organization, or its output. This is reflective of perceptions about the difference between this type of organization and a mixed-gender type, a distinction of which members of the group are keenly aware. This concern with process indicates that even in a group in which awareness of process is very strong, constraints on getting work done within it are an issue. Some women seem to suggest that this is a natural evolution of the organization:

> In the peace group we wanted a real sense of community. Initially we were more concerned about this than we are now. There has been a kind of natural evolution. We used to constantly talk about process and we don't do that so much anymore. Part of it is that we are so used to operating this way that we don't think about it. But also we do less process stuff. We used to go around the room at the beginning of a meeting and find out how everyone was, and we don't really do that anymore. . . . I think there is a push for efficiency. There may be a difference in style among the members of the group now.

The reference here to a difference in "style" in the membership is reflected in other statements as well. Some of the women indicate that they think the group has become less radical than it once was, meaning that it has settled into work on community-oriented projects rather than the kind of activist/protest activity it centered on during the Seneca Falls peace encampment. It seems that newer members, or those who were not directly involved in the founding of the group, are less concerned about process and more with task accomplishment. One

member who has been in the organization for four years and was not
a founding member offered the following comments:

> Recently there has been a greater emphasis on getting tasks done
> than the social aspect of the meetings. I don't feel good about it
> because I have contributed to that. That's partly my orientation—
> to get things done. There is a difference of opinion of how we should
> spend meeting time. We've tried to come up with ways to resolve
> it by saying, "Let's spend the first hour doing task-oriented things
> and the other hour discussing an issue or topic." I'm not part of
> the group for the social hour aspect. There is no question that they
> are good friends, but I go because there is something else I want
> to get out of it.

What is interesting about this person's comments is that she recognizes her own orientation toward working in the organization, but at
the same time recognizes the need for the social aspect or process-
oriented time. She further explained:

> I think this [emphasis on tasks] is because of changing membership.
> Redirection is a model of a task-oriented approach and I have won-
> dered if the people not doing redirection might have been won-
> dering, "What is it I am doing?" when in fact they were contributing
> the glue that keeps the organization together. I don't think that was
> recognized because the products of redirection are very visible and
> the glue that keeps an organization together is not.

There seems to be a recognition by this person that the organization
needs to find the right balance between these two elements. That was
less of a question for founding members, who felt that process was
most important and output could be sacrificed. Thus, there is a sense
that the organization has evolved by developing a structure and mod-
ifying the process. One woman who is no longer a member of the
active group said she enjoyed going to meetings because of the discussion of peace-related issues. Sometimes guest speakers would come,
but time would be set aside for theoretical kinds of discussions too.
She also indicated that the group was spontaneous in forming committees around issues:

> There used to be more ad hoc committees. Now we have evolved
> into more set committees. We used to discuss issues more at meet-
> ings. We've had less time for that. But we are still a consensus group.

At the time the peace group was studied, the trend toward task
accomplishment had not seriously threatened group process. Yet the

question seemed to loom large. At what point does task accomplishment become so important that it alters the process? At what point does an altered process hamper the group's ability to operate in non-hierarchical ways? In the time frame within which this organization was studied, these questions remained unsettled.

SUMMARY OF FINDINGS

There does not appear to be either a formal or informal hierarchy within the peace group. While there is a core active group that makes policy for the organization, this group is not engaged in handing down decisions to other members. The active group communicates with the supporting and sponsoring members in a way that allows them to participate whenever they wish and in whatever way they define their own participation. Any member of the organization may contribute to policy making at any time. Observation of activities at meetings suggested that no one person or group of persons attempted to dominate decision making. As one member explained, "In this group I don't see anyone who wants to take on power. I don't see any desire on the part of anyone to 'run' the organization." While organization members recognize that an informal hierarchy could develop, they believe that it will not, because the process they utilize, especially consensus decision making, prevents it.

Members of the organization show a high degree of commitment to the anarchist feminist goals of building alternative forms of organization. Of the active and supporting members interviewed, all expressed a commitment to the development of non-hierarchical structure within a feminist context or framework. The basic operating principles identified within this type of organization are consensus, empowerment, and emerging leadership. These principles are not new to the study of organizations. What is new is the way in which anarchist feminists put these principles together in order to build non-hierarchical organization structure. The uniqueness of the structure comes from the way in which it differs from purely consensual organization, in which all members must participate in all decisions. While the peace group began as purely consensual, it has evolved toward an increased emphasis on accomplishing tasks, as well as working on community-based projects rather than on those that included more radical protest behavior. In part, new members, more interested than the founding members in community-oriented projects and task accomplishment, contributed to this change. Task accomplishment versus process in the organization continues to be an issue for peace group members. Organization structure has begun to reflect this increasing concern.

In the interests of time, and task accomplishment, this organization decided to develop project groups that would make decisions and engage in activity in specific issue areas that had been determined by the larger group. Thus, they began to distinguish between critical and routine decisions, delegating routine decisions to project groups.[8]

However, the entire active group, including project group members, makes decisions on critical policy, while the smaller project groups make routine decisions in their work on tasks. For example, the active group decided to work toward increasing public awareness of the harmful effects of children's war toys. That decision, made by the entire active group, constitutes critical policy. It determines the organization's overall direction. The decision was made by consensus, utilizing the concept of process as previously described. Project group members, who also participated in this critical decision, decided the routine matters of what, specifically, they would do in the war toys context. The media project group, Redirection, decided to write a number of radio ads against war toys; these they recorded and had played by local stations. This was routine decision making.

An additional factor that peace group members believe enhances their ability to operate in non-hierarchical ways is their gender; they believe women are better listeners, better communicators, and less inclined to want to dominate decision-making processes than men. Thus, the female peace group members believe they are particularly skilled at the kind of process, structure, and potential for successful outcomes that constitute a feminist framework for organization.[9]

NOTES

1. Peace group, *Mission Statement*.
2. Peace and Justice Center *Newsletter*.
3. Peace group, *Mission Statement*.
4. The peace group conducted a telephone survey that showed these ads to be highly effective in the local listening area.
5. Joyce Rothschild and J. Allen Whitt, *The Cooperative Workplace* (Cambridge: Cambridge University Press, 1986), p. 51.
6. The small New England city in which this organization exists is itself homogeneous, with a less than 2 percent minority population. This accounts in part for the lack of racial diversity in these women's groups.
7. Rothschild and Whitt, p. 194.

8. Use of the terms "critical" and "routine" with regard to decisions was derived from the language of the women interviewed. However, it is also terminology that has been developed by Selznick and cited earlier in this study.

9. Again, it should be emphasized that this study is not designed to speak to the question of gender-related values. This part of the study simply reports what the women of the peace group believed to be true.

SIX

The Women's Health Collective

The Women's Health Collective was formed in 1972 in response to a need, voiced by a coalition of community members, for a facility to provide abortion and other health care services to women. In the spring of 1972, state law that had outlawed abortion was struck down by the state's supreme court. Shortly thereafter, in 1973, the U.S. Supreme Court made abortion legal in *Roe v. Wade*.

Various groups in this small New England city, including doctors, other health advocates, and feminist organizations, as well as concerned individuals, both male and female, held a meeting and elected a board of directors and working committees to help establish a clinic. During the summer of 1972, necessary resources in the form of money, space, equipment, doctors, and staff were gathered in order to begin provisionary abortions and health care services, including a wide range of gynecological care. When the center officially opened on September 1, 1972, it was the first health care center of its kind in the United States. Initially, the clinic met with political opposition in the community, generating negative attention. The clinic has continued to operate despite political pressure from hostile groups throughout its twenty years of experience.

HISTORY

The collective's history indicates that the demand for abortions in the first year was high, and resource limitations precluded establishment of other gynecological services.[1] As laws in other states, as well as nationally, changed to permit legalized abortions, the demand for abortion services at this particular clinic diminished. As a result, the clinic was able to develop a range of other services, including contraception counseling and diagnosis and treatment of women's reproductive disorders. These concerns, as well as abortion services, remain the major focus of the organization.

The organization has gone through at least two major structural changes since 1972. As explained, in its written history, "At the time of incorporation, a separate board of directors was established, with the staff meeting weekly to make decisions about the day-to-day running of the clinic, and the board meeting with the staff every two weeks to make major policy decisions." By September of 1974, the separate board of directors had become what the staff of the clinic refers to as a "technical legality." At the annual meeting that year the board voted to dissolve itself and the staff became the board. The staff elects officers of the board to satisfy the requirements of their non-profit, legal-corporate status but these women hold no special authority.

During the period from 1974 to 1986, the organization's philosophy was based on the idea that, ideally, each staff member should be trained to do any given task. Most staff members rotated counseling-related tasks and attended training programs to learn about specialized lab work and administrative skills such as medical protocol and physician assistant skills. The staff had an overlapping schedule of training periods to train members as physician's assistants. As explained in the organization's written history, "ideally, this orientation of medical care delivery helps to break down traditional roles and perceptions of doctors while reducing costs and expanding personalized quality medical care."[2]

The Women's Health Collective is a tax-exempt organization. It receives some contributions and a few grants for the purpose of training physician's assistants. The organization's primary source of income is derived from fees for services, with abortion services carrying a disproportionately large share of the income lost on other services. The written history notes that "no one is pleased with this relationship, and the staff has tried several ways to alter the situation. Twenty percent of the women seen are partially covered under Medicaid. There is a sliding fee scale based on one's ability to pay, and over one-third of the patients are subsidized to some extent."[3]

The size of the health center staff has varied throughout the years, at its largest between 1974 and 1981, during which time approximately twenty women, including three physicians and six physician's assistants, worked three to five days a week. While the background, education, and ages of the women vary to some extent, in general they have been from thirty to fifty years old and white middle class. This is not surprising, since the community in which the organization exists cannot be described as economically or racially diverse.

The Women's Health Collective's facilities have changed over the years as a result of both planned and unplanned circumstances. The organization began in a small facility outside the city's downtown area. In 1974 the staff realized more room would be needed and moved to an office building. Downtown space was renovated by a crew of women carpenters. In 1977, however, this entire building was destroyed by fire, and the health collective lost nearly everything. Nonetheless the staff was able to find temporary space in the downtown area and continued gynecological services through Planned Parenthood. Income from these services was enough to keep the organization solvent while it tried to rebuild. By July of 1977, the clinic had purchased a house in the city's north end, renovated it, and opened its full range of services. During this period staff members willingly worked as volunteers and ran a temporary clinic while also helping to renovate the house that continues as its operating location.

The staff went through another major structural change in 1986, resulting in the organization's current structure. A highlight of this change was the development of coordinator positions. The need for these positions surfaced out of years of discussion about decision making in the group and the need to become more efficient as a business. The positions were designed to reflect the special knowledge and expertise of certain members. Responsibility for routine decisions was delegated to four women in the areas of personnel, medical, business, and outreach. In addition, a coordinator-at-large position rotates among interested members. The coordinators meet weekly as a group to discuss their various concerns and activities. There is also a personnel committee made up of five members including the personnel coordinator, who is elected by the rest of the board (described below). While the entire staff participates in personnel decisions such as hiring, firing, and determination of salaries, the personnel committee helps to establish criteria for those decisions. The staff refers to this new structure as a "modified collective."

OPERATING PROCEDURES

The Women's Health Collective has six major areas of responsibility. These are the board of directors, comprised of the full staff; the personnel committee; coordinators; practitioner meetings; counselor meetings; and area coordinator meetings.

Board/Staff

To be a voting board member, a staff member must be a regularly scheduled worker at sixteen hours or more per week, eight of which must be clinic work and none of which can include board meeting time. The board member must make a one-year commitment to this minimum weekly schedule. One may also choose to become a non-voting board member. New employees hired with a minimum regular schedule of sixteen hours or more per week attend meetings as non-voting members prior to making a one-year commitment at the time of their three-month evaluation. All persons meeting these criteria may elect to be on the board, but they are not required to do so. Board members have responsibility for attending monthly meetings of the staff board and for final approval by consensus vote of many critical policy decisions.[4] Consensus vote is defined by the organization as follows: "Consensus means each individual agrees with the decision on a group level." The areas in which the full staff/board makes decisions are as follows:

1. hiring and firing of employees
2. decisions that set new directions structurally, medically, politically, or financially
3. fee setting and staff salaries
4. fiscal budget (yearly)
5. large capital expenses outside of budget
6. election of coordinator-at-large (yearly)
7. election of Personnel Committee members
8. staff evaluations
9. coordinator appointments
10. structure evaluation.

The purpose of board meetings is described as follows:

1. approval of the business issues described above
2. forum for updates from medical, outreach, personnel, and business areas

3. forum for recommendations from the coordinators
4. delegation of tasks to the Coordinator Group
5. setting, evaluating, and contributing to new health center directions.

In addition, staff/board members have the following privileges:

1. Any board member may serve on a hiring or personnel committee, take on a delegated task, or participate in new service development by putting in a request to personnel and receiving approval by the board.
2. Any board member may request election to the coordinator group as its at-large member.

Personnel Committee

The personnel committee consists of five members including the coordinator. Members are elected by the staff/board at the beginning of a new fiscal year and are not confined to a maximum length of term. They serve six hours of administrative time monthly, including two or more regular monthly meetings. The tasks of the committee are as follows:

1. create personnel policy
2. design and maintain systems for staff evaluations and structure evaluations
3. hear and make recommendations on grievances, new requests, or training requests
4. organize and initiate hiring and send three members to serve on the hiring committee
5. delegate administrative job assignments and time assignments
6. recommend raises and decisions on hiring and firing to the full staff/board.

In general, any new recommendations in any area go to the coordinator group for discussion and approval. If the group does not approve it, they send the issue back to personnel. If the two groups cannot agree, they go to the full staff/board for a vote. Any decisions that would initiate a direction change, meaning a change in the key objectives of the clinic, must be approved by the board.

Coordinator Group

The coordinator group is comprised of five individuals charged with the following tasks:

1. identify, design, and implement new services
2. prepare yearly fiscal budget
3. review clinic income needs
4. report to staff on research and development of new services
5. set direction
6. coordinate advertising, doctor searches, and fund raising
7. plan annual staff/board meeting on budget
8. manage investments and evaluate the need for new projects, keeping the clinic on firm financial ground
9. review applications that have a potential for new services
10. review training requests
11. troubleshoot legal issues
12. assess hiring needs and make recommendations to staff.

This group meets weekly and each member is paid for four hours per week. The group provides weekly minutes of its meeting to all other staff members and elicits feedback, reporting all appropriate issues directly to the board. Area coordinators are elected by the board and reappointed yearly; they are subject to review by the board. Vacant coordinator positions are opened to staff before being advertised externally. The role of each coordinator is described below.

Personnel Coordinator. The personnel coordinator has the delegated tasks of maintaining and updating personnel policies, responding to incoming job applications, and preparing the payroll. The job duties can be described as follows:

1. Coordinating and maintaining evaluation systems
2. Scheduling and coordinating special/new projects
3. Monitoring time and benefits
4. Liaison activities with staff regarding schedule and personnel policies
5. Coordinating counseling service
6. Preparing fiscal budget
7. Coordinating and delegating training
8. Scheduling patient visits and workers;
9. Planning new services involving personnel decisions
10. Coordinating personnel committee
11. Clinic trouble shooting
12. Assigning new clinic task assignments
13. Assessing hiring needs
14. Reviewing incoming job applications.

Medical Coordinator. The medical coordinator has the delegated tasks of auditing all lab activities, updating the staff with medical research and maintaining a medical library, training of medical personnel, developing new services, and supervising medical inventory. The job includes the following tasks:

1. Coordinating audit of lab, as well as training outside medical personnel and staff
2. Medical research, protocol update and maintenance
3. Medical backup for clinic workers
4. Liaison with community medical board
5. Quality assurance of medical personnel
6. Coordinating training, referrals and workshops, and practitioner and counselor meetings
7. Inventory, including ordering and evaluating new medical books and pamphlets.

Business Coordinator. The business coordinator has the delegated tasks of maintaining accounts receivable and accounts payable, preparing monthly statements, creating the fiscal yearly budget, and preparing material for accounts. This person also serves as a liaison with service workers and coordinates inventory, building maintenance, mail, and other errands. The job includes the following:

1. Maintaining accounts receivable and accounts payable
2. Creating payroll tax reports
3. Monitoring investments
4. Preparing monthly statements
5. Yearly reviewing of insurance plans and needs
6. Yearly preparing and gathering of reports for workman's compensation and malpractice
7. Preparing material for audit of records
8. Preparing yearly budget
9. Liaison with bank for special projects
10. Participating in planning new services from the financial side
11. Monitoring financial solvency and status
12. Researching and recommending on capital expenditures
13. Overseeing budget and approving ongoing capital expenditures
14. Coordinating building maintenance.

Outreach Coordinator. The outreach coordinator has the delegated tasks of coordinating speaking engagements; participating in local, state, regional, and national organizations, and at health fairs; and maintaining a mailing list of other organizations. She is assigned the following tasks:

1. Sharing information and updating staff on political issues
2. Coordinating speaking engagements/health fairs
3. Troubleshooting legal issues, liaison with attorney
4. Liaison with lobbyist, networking with legislators
5. Coordinating media representation of the clinic
6. Participating in local, state, and national health/political organizations
7. Politically representing the clinic to medical bureaucracies
8. Liaison with the board of medical practice
9. Monitoring political strategies and setting direction.

Coordinator-At-Large. The coordinator-at-large participates in coordinator group meetings and shares in the general coordinator tasks described earlier rather than undertaking specific area tasks and concerns.

Practitioner Meetings And Counselor Meetings

These groups meet monthly to recommend, review, and update protocol in their respective areas; to approve new resources; to cut down on medical discrepancies among physician's assistants; and to perform a "chart review"—or review of medical case histories—of individuals. Meetings are designed to review and improve medical services continually.

Other Positions

In addition to the various positions and roles described above, nearly everyone in the collective performs the tasks of either health advocate or physician's assistant. The health advocate is a health educator. This person serves as main desk receptionist, takes patient histories, and does counseling with regard to contraception and other medical information. It is not a "hands on" role within the clinic, and thus no specific training is required by the state.

Physician's assistants are hands on and must go through an apprenticeship training program approved by the state. The health collective has a registered training plan arrangement with the state which is comprised of a three-year program with academic requirements, including a verbal and written exam. The health collective is currently the only organization with a program recognized by the state. At the time of this study there were seven physician's assistants on staff, only one of whom was trained at a facility other than the health collective.

In addition to these positions, the health collective has an arrangement with an outside counseling practice that offers private psychological counseling. One or two counselors from this practice meet with patients at the clinic who have requested their services. Outside counselors attend staff/board meetings once a month to give feedback or to offer important insights or concerns to the staff regarding the operation of the clinic.

ANALYSIS

The story of the Women's Health Collective is the story of an organization attempting to address the problems of consensual organization prevalent in the 1960s and early '70s by developing a modified consensual structure. This organization was born out of a "consciousness-raising" period of feminism. A major focus of the time was the emergence of women into the work force, gaining control over their lives economically, politically, and socially. This movement embraced the right to control one's body, including the right to choose abortion.

The health collective reflected these changes both in style of organization and services offered. The collective was organized around a need for safe abortions in the community and derived much of its early financial and community support from this service. At the same time, the organization was providing an avenue for women in the community to change their roles, to work outside the home and develop new interests and skills while contributing to political and social change. While the organization was initially formed by both men and women concerned about women's reproductive rights, it soon developed into a women-run operation. As noted, just two years after its inception, the board as such was dissolved, leaving the women who had been running the clinic through consensus-based decision making on their own.

In the staff-run consensual structure, many of the women in the organization worked only part-time, some as volunteers. Many either had other sources of income from spouses or family members or had limited needs because they were students who shared housing. For many, it was their first "real" job outside home; they were concerned that they might not know enough about what they were trying to do. As one woman recounts, "This was my first job, my first board, my first everything . . . and I had no experience with it."

Yet there were some within the group, particularly those centered around the primary medical activity of the clinic, who did have expertise and were responsible for teaching and sharing information with other members. Initially, two doctors also worked in the clinic providing abortion services. These services would later be limited to two days a week, with the physicians working part-time. In other words, doctors would not be on hand in the clinic except on abortion days.

From 1974 to 1981 the clinic was a truly consensual organization. In terms of job title, no one person held any more responsibility or authority than another with regard to decision making. The full staff/board met once a week to discuss all decisions, no matter how small or large. Decisions were made by consensus, meaning that everyone had to be able to "live with or agree to" the decision. If even one person objected, the subject would be discussed and possibly tabled until the next meeting. On some occasions, however, if division on an issue persisted, some combination of consensus and voting would be used as a last resort.

What is of great interest about the collective is how it evolved from this consensual structure, with no vertical or horizontal differentiation of position or financial reward, to the modified consensual structure it had at the time of this study. It is interesting to consider the types of external and internal constraints that led the organization to the point of structural change. Externally, these constraints were related to the changing role of women as well as to attitudes toward a range of values related to earning money and gaining prestige. Other external considerations were related to changes in the medical/health care field and to political/state requirements about administration of health care. Internal constraints appeared to be size, financial solvency, and the general needs of workers for job satisfaction and reward. To some extent, these external and internal constraints were interrelated. This became apparent through discussion with the women of the organization as they explained how the organization evolved.

It is important to recognize that the women of the health collective speak not only as organization members but also as employees. Interviews with these women focus directly on the structural changes the organization has undergone. While these women, like those of the peace group, emphasize the importance of consensual procedures or process as it was defined in the previous chapter, discussion of the health collective will center on definition and description of what they call a "modified consensual structure." Specifically, discussion will fall

under two major headings: emerging from consensual organization
and development of a modified consensual structure.

Emerging From Consensual Organization

Discussion surrounding the move toward a modified consensual
structure highlights the concerns or problems that the women of the
health collective experienced with the fully consensual structure. Interviews indicate that these problems centered on questions of efficiency in running a solvent business and providing quality health care.
The change to a modified consensual structure resulted from experience within the organization, but was confirmed by a conscious decision to change official structures to reflect new ones that had developed already.

Efficiency. Concerns over efficiency stemmed primarily from what was
identified in the last chapter as the consensual process. This process
is comprised of consensus decision making, the notion of empowerment, and rotation of jobs. In the consensual process, everyone participated in every decision, no matter how large or small. Over time,
organization members began to experience the costs involved in maintaining a business this way. One member explained:

> I think it was just impossible to have twenty-two people [at that time]
> run a business that employed twenty-two people. I think because of
> the nature of the way this business was, and is, that it could not
> continue to operate as a collective because decisions have to be made
> quickly sometimes, and no one had the power to make those de-
> cisions.

Rotation of jobs at the health collective also became a problem related to efficiency within the organization. Members indicated that the
costs of rotation were high, in terms of retraining, keeping skilled
people, and maintaining a degree of job satisfaction among workers.
One woman explained it this way:

> There was a real problem in terms of someone building and grow-
> ing in certain job descriptions and having a certain area of expertise
> when somebody else could come along and say she wants your job.
> It wasn't giving any job security to those who had been here for
> years and were doing a good job and, again, it was inefficient in
> terms of financial cost [retraining].

Another problem with rotation of jobs involved hiring new people to move eventually into any position. This, the women indicated, is still a problem under the new structure. But under the old structure it created a double concern, about lack of job security and about expectations surrounding new members' abilities to perform as well as older members had in those jobs. As one of the coordinators explained:

> In that situation there is no sense of job security for the person who has been there and the new person coming in is in a pretty difficult position in terms of kicking you out of your job *and* being able to perform at your capacity.

What developed in the case of new members, and even those members already there and seeking to move into new positions, was a "selective" rotation. One coordinator put it this way:

> In a case where someone's job performance in an area was questionable, the group allowed the rotation to happen. When someone was doing a good job, it was harder for the group to support that rotation. If someone lost a job they were really interested in, it was sometimes hard for them to remain at the clinic. And then it was difficult for the staff to support someone new coming in and doing that job.

Other problems with the consensual structure centered around recognition of expertise or skill of individuals in particular jobs. Women in the organization began to want recognition in the form of job permanency and a salary reflecting their skills and experience. One woman explained it this way:

> As the political structures moved more away from collectives and more into the late '70s and early '80s, we moved with that. I think people recognized that it was O.K. to make money, it was O.K. to have authority that was given by the group. In our organization that was happening, but it wasn't being recognized or rewarded financially. The group was giving responsibility to certain women, but the group wasn't recognizing it was doing that, and the women were feeling used.

As this statement indicates, part of the change taking place in the organization was a change in thinking regarding earnings. Reality for many of the women who continued to work in the collective was a need for full-time work to support a family; they could no longer continue as part-time employees with part-time salaries. This change stemmed from environmental factors: the changing role of women in society, a nationwide record high divorce rate, and an increase in the number of single women heading households.

> With regard to the salary issue, in the beginning most people worked part-time and either had someone else supporting them or low-level needs. More of the people then did not rely on this place as a primary place of support. Then more people started to work full-time and salary became an issue.

It becomes apparent that many issues are interrelated in the health collective's emergence from a consensual structure to a modified consensual structure. The need for increased full-time salaries, recognition of skills and expertise, and smaller staff size raised questions of efficiency. The connections-among these issues are demonstrated by the following statement:

> The change [to the new structure] came about through a combination of the salary issue and wanting some kind of formal authority to do the job you were doing. Part of the problem was you would do this work and you would bring it to the staff and they would question if you did this or that. It didn't give you job satisfaction. There was resentment on both sides: the people doing the work were working without recognition and the other side thought there was power-mongering going on in secret. The old structure worked for that time, but things have changed and it started to work less efficiently. We realized we were in the business world. Some of the business problems centered around not having so large a staff and trying to operate more efficiently so we would see the same amount of people with less staff.

When asked about efficiency and the structural change, another woman responded this way:

> I think it was a long process. Some of it had to do with responsibility around abortions and malpractice. Some wanted to stay in administrative positions. It was to our advantage not to take so long in the process of making decisions. The change was initiated by people who wanted to get paid better and thought it would work better.

Changes in Political Ideals. What brought the health collective to the point of amending its consensual structure was an eventual recognition that environmental conditions, both inside and outside the organization, were changing. The organization needed to identify those changes and adjust accordingly to survive. The process the health collective went through is an example of adaptation to environment and highlights the importance of the impact of environmental constraints on internal structure. In order to identify these constraints and the changes occurring because of them, the collective hired an outside evaluator. The evaluator, a feminist woman from the local area who was a trained counselor, facilitated a number of meetings over a two-year period prior to the structural change, to aid members in speaking freely about what they thought should change in the organization's structure.

It became clear that over time, the membership of the health collective had become what one member described as "less radical." She explained, "I think a lot of radical women who worked here are no longer here. . . . In order for the clinic to survive we've had to become more mainstream, and I think a radical establishment does not last." The use of the word radical here does not refer to radical feminism as defined in Part I of this research, but instead to a common understanding of "radical" as deviating from the norm and engaging in protest activities.

To survive, the health collective had to be viewed as more mainstream by the rest of the community. The organization had to establish its legitimacy in the community as well as with its own members. As one member explained, "We are a well over a quarter-of-a-million-dollar-a-year business, and we haven't taken ourselves seriously." Getting "serious" about the business was one important aspect of the structural change. It appeared to require women of the collective to make business a priority at the expense of consensual process. It required a shift in political ideals. As one woman explained, "The change involved people letting go of their ideologies around the way the collective should be, the way women are, letting go of the idea of collectives working." Again, as in the last chapter, there is some indication that these women believe there is a relationship between collective ideals and those of women, that women can be more successful in this kind of structure. The comment about "the way women are" also reflects a conflict between how the women would like the organization to work and the realities of the business world.

Another aspect of this change in political ideals relates to new membership. As women in the organization began working full-time, and the organization shrank in size, members became more interested in the organization as a business, and more women were attracted who shared this interest. As one woman indicated, "Some people left and the people who stayed were more interested in the business as a profession." However, these women were still very committed to feminist goals. The group, over time, became less anarchist feminist on the issue of structure and more liberal feminist. As another member explained:

> I don't think it has compromised the political goals. I think the way we are we're still a political feminist organization. I think we are not out in the streets creating a lot of havoc because the demand is here [meaning the clinic]. . . . What we have done is grown as a business—become more visible. I think our politics center around abortion and it takes a tremendous amount of energy. . . . I think we are very feminist. We're a lot tighter [as an] organization.

While this quote illustrates some movement away from anarchist goals to a more mainstream position, it makes clear that the movement is marginal. These women have not abandoned anarchist goals, but have modified them according to business interests and an interest in the organization's survival. Had they abandoned their original ideals altogether, they simply would have created a hierarchy and not worried about consensual process. Yet there is no indication within the organization that the structure will become hierarchical.

> What I perceive happening to this clinic is that it is not going to move on to another level. I think we have gone from a collectively to a semi-structured business where all the workers have a tremendous amount of control.

Development of the Modified Structure

The modified consensual structure attempts to resolve the problems of the consensual structure as discussed above. Chief among those problems was a need for efficient decision making and the recognition of expertise through salary increments and permanency in specific jobs. Thus, the coordinator positions were created.

The Coordinator Positions. As described earlier in this chapter, the health collective developed five initial coordinator positions to reflect medical, personnel, business, and political expertise of members. As the women of the organization describe it, the process through which these positions emerged was one of recognizing expertise already present in the group, but not recognized through differential salaries and job permanency. Thus, as it was explained, the new structure confirmed expertise already existing, and jobs that individuals had developed for themselves. As one of the coordinators explained:

> In my opinion, what the new structure did was formalize and put down on paper what was happening already, that in the collective it is not totally flat. Different people for different reasons take on more responsibility and have more degrees of power. They have more levels of information and have different work styles. That creates a less than flat structure. Some of what we did was bring our definition of the structure to a more realistic point—more to what was really happening.

Other coordinators reflected the same concept of emerging leadership, or bringing the organization's structure in line with the way members had defined their own roles. The following examples illustrate this point:

> I think the organization changed formally, recently. I think that the organization has been evolving informally as any active, alive group evolves. We identified the changes and give them names. But I think the change was always happening.

> What happened over time was that the group we are working with now kind of settled. Everyone settled in the place [job] they wanted to be in, with still some areas of growth.

One member, who was on the board before it was abolished, explained how the coordinator positions began to develop within the organization.

> The coordinator's group started with a number of people who were willing to spend more time, who rapped together and did a lot of discussion of the clinic after hours. They were possibly more interested. They were already doing the coordinator jobs and they needed to be recognized.

This statement indicates that some kind of subgroup existed within the collective from early on in the organization. This reality is reflected in at least one interview with one of the coordinators. She explained that:

> While we were still a flat structure, people perceived. . . . power groups and the power groups took some knocking for that. What I got out of that, and I think we came full circle, is that the group put people in that position. It is not just that we are there because we choose to be, but the group devises subgroups and puts people in power. The group hands out responsibility and needs people to

play different roles. It is a combination of your wanting [the position] for yourself but also the group empowering you with that.

This discussion indicates that organization members wanted to recognize individuals with valuable expertise and give them legitimacy. They wanted leadership and people with some degree of authority over specific areas. Without identifying these people and their roles, there was a perception among members of a lack of control. One woman explained the relationship between the coordinators and the rest of the group in this way:

> Right now we have three people sitting in coordinator positions where they are in charge of their areas. I don't think those three people or the people not in those positions would want to eliminate those positions. This is because these positions are our way of hanging on to the reins of the business and having some control.

Again, the perceived need for people to be in charge of certain areas, to exercise control over the business, reflects the organization's need for expertise and some permanency in positions in order to respond to business needs and organizational maintenance. (Under the new structure, only the coordinator's positions are permanent. All other jobs rotate.)

Routine Versus Critical Decisions. Given this emerging leadership within the group and the designation of coordinator positions that do not rotate, the question arises as to the relationship of coordinators to the rest of the members making decisions. Again, designation of coordinators had at least two major purposes: recognition of expertise, and the need for efficiency and control over business matters. This development of a coordinating group led to a distinction between the decisions coordinators would make and those made by the entire group. The role of trust was one important element in the new structure. Some of the women explained:

> We trust the people who sit in those roles. They represent us, they make recommendations to us, yet they are part of us. They can't change the direction of the collective politically, financially, or medically.

> The people who are sitting in those positions are people I can trust, who the group has a good relationship with and believes do a good job.

It should be pointed out that this is the product of what previously has been called process, and that the group is homogeneous and of a similar mindset. Under these circumstances, delegation of responsibility may be less threatening. Additionally, there exists faith in the process. As one woman pointed out, "Every member sitting in a coordinator's role is evaluated by staff members and every member has the right to dismiss any coordinator. I don't see their positions as power. I see them as tedious responsibility."

Delegation of responsibility is based on distinctions among decisions. Those that are critical have the potential for changing the organization's direction, while those that are routine are important to the daily operation of the business but not likely to raise significant questions about policy changes. This distinction, as discussed in Part I of this study, is crucial to implementation and maintenance of decentralized organizations, because it sets up the structure for maintaining authority at the organization's center while still allowing for delegation of responsibility to lower levels. It is important to compare the use of the critical-versus-routine distinction in decentralized organizations with its use in the Women's Health Collective.

In a decentralized setting that is clearly hierarchical, critical decisions are reserved for those at the top level of the organization, while routine decisions are delegated downward. This is thought to be useful for at least two reasons. First, personnel at lower levels who are delegated responsibility deal with problems they are close to and have information about. It is assumed they have the resources to make whatever the organization defines as effective decisions at this level. Second, executives who are freed from routine decision making have more time to consider large policy questions that will ultimately determine the direction of the organization.[5]

In the health collective, critical decisions are reserved for the entire membership of the organization, while routine decisions are delegated horizontally to the coordinators (see figure 6–1). Like those at lower levels in a decentralized structure, coordinators make decisions relating to problems they are close to and have information about. An example of this would be the decision a medical coordinator makes as to whether the clinic should use disposable (plastic) medical supplies or those that are reusable but must be disinfected in an autoclave. A decision of this kind may change procedures within the clinic, and possibly affect the budget in a minor way, but does not affect the overall direction of the organization.

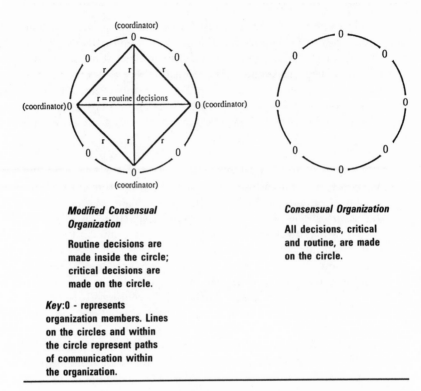

(coordinator)

r = routine decisions

(coordinator) 0

0 (coordinator)

(coordinator)

Modified Consensual Organization

Routine decisions are made inside the circle; critical decisions are made on the circle.

Consensual Organization

All decisions, critical and routine, are made on the circle.

Key:**0 - represents organization members. Lines on the circles and within the circle represent paths of communication within the organization.**

Figure 6.1. Consensual and Modified Consensual Organization.

Routine decisions have the potential to become critical, at which point they can be reconsidered by the entire group. For instance, if the decision in the above example was to use an autoclave to disinfect equipment but clinic workers were not doing this correctly and patients were becoming infected, the issue would become critical, because it would threaten the organization's survival if not dealt with effectively. As in the decentralized structure, those members of the health collective freed of routine decisions have time to consider large policy questions about organizational direction.

One important difference between a hierarchical decentralized structure and that of the health collective is that only a few people in the decentralized structure, those at the top of the hierarchy, make critical policy. In the health collective, everyone together, including the coordinators, makes critical policy as members of the organization. Thus, coordinators take part in all critical decisions and some routine decisions in their designated area of expertise. Other members make only critical decisions. In this way coordinators have additional responsibility, and authority, in their areas of expertise. But this responsibility, authority, and expertise does not appear to result in a hierarchical arrangement. Nevertheless, coordinators carry more responsibility than other members and are paid more for it.

One member of the organization explained the new structure this way:

> We are down to three coordinators now, who are making smaller decisions that the whole group shouldn't spend time on. Before the coordinator positions were created, everybody had to make every decision in weekly staff meetings. Now the coordinator group can make the more routine decisions. With the larger decisions, the co-ordinator group can discuss it all they want, but it has to go to the larger group. But a lot of problems get worked out in the smaller group. A lot of times issues will be brought up and we are asked to think about them. It may not all be decided in the same day. We may discuss it and then wait another month before we really decide. We didn't use to do that; we used to discuss it to death.

This woman goes on to explain the way she views this arrangement: "No one is 'working for' anyone else" in the organization. She adds that it is inappropriate, in her view, to think of coordinator positions as administratively above or below the rest of the members. She believes that everyone works on the same level and coordinators "interact" with the rest of the members.

In describing the new structure, members of the organization had difficulty deciding what to call it. They could explain how it works, but struggled to find appropriate language. Some called it a semi-structure or a modified collective or simply said they think the structure is not "flat" and therefore not a collective any longer. Some members used the word hierarchy, but it is interesting to note that these women contradicted such a definition in their explanations of how the organization actually works. One coordinator offered the following insights:

> I could be more traditional than this [new structure] allows. I could be more hierarchical. I still have an issue, I still have a problem, with the amount of responsibility I have and lack of authority. I have more responsibility than I did before the structure changed. My position feels *very* responsible. I am the primary medical person when a doctor is not here, which is more often since we no longer have a doctor on staff but instead contract out for one. Because of

this, my position changed more than anyone else's with the structural change. Other coordinators say they are getting paid what they are worth. I haven't approached that.

This woman clearly perceives the limits of her authority under the new structure. She seems to want a hierarchy and is frustrated that she does not have one. She worries about being accountable for medical decisions, but not having the authority to carry them out.

The business coordinator echoed this problem of lack of authority. She also indicated that some of the decisions she sees as routine are still made by the full staff.

> Theoretically, the staff/board is supposed to talk only about large financial expenditures or decisions that are going to affect the business as far as changing the direction. Realistically, that is not exactly what happens. For instance, one coordinator is leaving. Rather than a coordinator's group saying we don't want to fill that position because the whole group has gotten smaller and it will be more efficient that way, the decision has to go to the whole group for discussion because it is a structural change. Wrong. The coordinator group should be able to say we don't need so many coordinators and save the group from having to make that decision.

This statement, as well as that of the medical coordinator indicates that the women in coordinator positions have a clear sense of the boundaries of their decision making. At times they are frustrated by these boundaries, and would like more authority than is provided by the new structure. This can be taken as one indication that the new structure in fact operates the way members have described it. However, it also indicates constraints in that coordinators perceive the need for more authority and would be willing to compromise anarchist feminist goals to change the structure.

MODIFIED STRUCTURE AND CONSENSUS

The modified structure still has many consensual elements to it. This becomes especially evident through two unique interviews: one with a new member of the organization who was dissatisfied and had decided to leave it, and another with a woman who had recently undergone an abortion at the health collective. The first interview indicates the degree to which the new structure had moved away from a purely consensual one. The second shows how much of consensual process remains. To demonstrate these points, these interviews are presented in a relatively complete form.

INTERVIEW 1: Dissatisfied Member

QUESTION: Why did you join this organization?
"I was real interested in working in a business run by women that offered services to women. But a lot of my expectations about what it was going to be like working here have not proven true. I expected when I came here that people would be real good at consensus decision making and improving ways of equalizing power. I arrived when the structure had been reorganized."

QUESTION: What is your sense of the kind of change that took place here?
"The change streamlined the structure against the tide of what I wanted. When I found out that people used to meet every week, that sounded more like what I wanted. The idea of having more of a hierarchy now, with a few women on the coordinating group making routine decisions and the rest of us finding that out every month and making the major decisions is not my first choice of how to do things."

QUESTION: How would you describe your expectations?
"Part of what I expected was a lot of emotional support. I'm not getting the kind of appreciation and emotional support I need. A lot of what I heard when I came here was 'we already tried that,' or 'that doesn't work,' because this is what happened before. I'm real process-oriented. They don't want that now and that's what I have to offer. Consensus is the only true way to equalize power. What I have to offer is being left out of the new system."

QUESTION: Do you think the organization's goals have been compromised through this structural change?
"I hear a small voice from a few women who have been here from the beginning saying we need to keep our vision, we need to keep our politics intact, we need to keep talking about these issues, and that voice is much smaller now than it has been before. The voice that is bigger is the one that says we need to progress economically as a business, we need to be able to make better money here, which is a feminist issue. We need to make better services to keep the door open. They have to overlap."

INTERVIEW 2: Abortion Patient

QUESTION: What made you decide to go to the Women's Health Collective rather than another facility?
"I thought I would feel more comfortable in an all-female setting, that there would be more sensitive care. On the other hand, I was asking myself if this was a real operation, if they were really qual-

ified health care providers. That fear was dispelled immediately by
the people working there. It was dispelled by their immediate
professionalism. They weren't officious, but just gave off the attitude that, yes, we are real health care professionals.

"I picked up on feminist ideals through the literature in the
building and things hanging on the wall, not through anything in
particular that was said or done. But I did get a different feeling
than I would from a more traditional health care setting. It is much
less hierarchical in the relationships that are going on with the health
care providers. I had no idea of who was a receptionist, who was a
counselor, midwife, or doctor. For a moment I was a little disori-
ented by it, asking myself, what are the qualifications of the people
here? But the professional manner in which they interacted with
me dispelled my confusion. I had a feeling it was a much more
cooperative working situation. Whether or not they actually shift
jobs so that one person is a receptionist and the other upstairs, you
had the sense they could do that and respected one another. I felt
totally comfortable there. If they are going to treat one another
with that respect, you know it is extended to you."

QUESTION: How did you find their counseling?
"It was not unprofessional and not a chat with your best friend. The
way women have of sharing felt perfectly natural but not folksy. It
is not that women are better caretakers. It is the process that women
are used to that extends itself into a professional organization. That
there is no sense of job titles doesn't get in the way of a sense that
they know what they are doing. They have confidence and clarity."

The first of these interviews clearly demonstrates the major point of
this analysis, that efficiency has become an increasing priority over
process. While many elements of consensual process remain as indicated by interviews and personal observation, they have not kept new
structure from making a difference, namely, shifting the balance of
influence to favor business aspects of the organization and its survival.
Yet the interview with the abortion client is an important indicator
that the organization has not abandoned its consensual foundation.
Process is still important; it remains a defining characteristic, resulting
from a feminist framework in practice.

SUMMARY OF FINDINGS

Important clues as to current methods of operation within the
Women's Health Collective come through discussion of recent change
from a consensual structure to one in which coordinator positions have

emerged. The women themselves, within this organization, struggle to find appropriate language to describe this new structure. Some call it a modified collective, some a semi-structure, and some a hierarchy.

What is most important, for this research, is the method by which hierarchy is distinguished from other possible forms of organization. It is useful to note again that hierarchy has been defined as "a vertical and horizontal system of domination with varying degrees of centralized communication, resulting in unequal authority." Interviews with women in this organization, as well as personal observation of meetings, demonstrates that these women believe authority to make decisions in critical areas of finance and overall direction rests with the total membership. This seems especially clear in interviews with coordinators, who all express frustration that they do not have more decision making power in their respective areas. Even women who use the word hierarchy to describe their organization follow up by explaining the difference between critical and routine decisions and who makes them. They indicate that coordinators do not make critical policy. This fact runs counter to a definition of hierarchy. Observation of meetings also indicates that no one person or group runs the show. Members are careful about process. Coordinators are respected for their expertise in their areas, and can be opinion leaders as a result; but neither observation nor interviews revealed the ability of coordinators to translate expertise into single authority to make critical decisions. The three current coordinators reflect on this situation as they talk about the limitations of their respective jobs.

A second point in distinguishing hierarchy from other forms of organization relates to the idea of vertical and horizontal divisions of labor. Women in the health collective do not conceive of their organization in these terms. They describe it as an interaction. The interview with a client confirms that at least one outsider could not determine rank or even specific job titles within the organization. There was also a perception of a broad range of knowledge among the women there, in that the client perceived jobs were or could be rotated. This also suggests that communication is not centralized in the coordinator's group, and flows mainly through the full staff at their monthly meetings. Other groups and committees meet, but the coordinator's group is not the clearing house for this information; the full staff is.

An important factor in the structural change appears to have been the change in women's needs and concerns over the period of time from 1973 to 1986 when the new structure was formed. As many of the women indicate, when the health collective was first organized, many of them did not have jobs outside the home, were not as concerned about salary, and could afford to volunteer. Times have changed. More women now want and need to have careers, due to increased accessibility to the professions, increased awareness of the benefits and rewards of careers including elevated self-esteem and a much increased need to earn good salaries to support their children as the primary wage earner. These are societal changes manifested within the health collective. A decrease in volunteer help and an increase in those women who wanted and needed to work full-time for better salaries, and who brought a liberal feminist approach to the organization, led the collective to develop a smaller but full-time, better paid staff. It also raised the issue of a pay scale, whereas prior to the change in structure, differentiation of pay did not exist. Salary came to be based on a combination of longevity and type of job performed.

Along with salary changes, there were business changes. As one coordinator put it, "A collective is an expensive way to run a business." To survive, the organization needed to become more efficient. This reality translated into fewer full staff meetings and delegation to coordinators of routine tasks, resulting in a swifter decision-making process. This turn of events meant sacrifices in process. In the past, part of every meeting was designed to bring a part of the personal lives of members into their organization. Most members indicate that this kind of support is no longer there, although some would like it to be. Interestingly, some members still view their organization as supportive—just not in staff meetings. Other members even find this support to distinguish them from other organizations. It is part of their feminist commitment, a framework within which they struggle to maintain a business with a non-hierarchical structure.

NOTES

1. Women's Health Collective, *History*, p. 9.
2. Ibid., p. 3.
3. Ibid.
4. The terminology of "critical" and "routine" decisions was used by organization members. Students of organization behavior attribute this terminology to the work of Philip Selznick in his book *Leadership in Administration*.
5. Selznick, pp. 56–64.

SEVEN

The Business Women's Group

The national organization of the business women's group was founded in 1919. This organization has a long tradition of supporting women's rights and goals in the workplace. The mission statement of this national organization is to promote "full participation, equality, and economic self-sufficiency for working women."[1] Its objectives are summarized as follows: to elevate the standards for women in business and the professions; to promote the interests of business and professional women; to bring about a spirit of cooperation among business and professional women of the United States; and to extend opportunities to business and professional women through education geared toward industrial, scientific, and vocational activities.[2]

The national organization also describes its "working objectives" as the following: to provide an environment in which personal development and career enhancement is encouraged through interaction among working women; to formulate, monitor, and influence laws, regulations, and policies that have an impact on working women; to lead in the collection, analysis, and dissemination of information for and about working women; and to address issues and create a structure that will attract a membership reflective of America's female labor force.[3] This organization indicates no commitment, within these working objectives, to any particular organizational structure or method of decision making. However, the organization's by-laws indicate the design for a formal hierarchy.

HISTORY

The business women's national organization was among the first to support a federal Equal Rights Amendment when it was first introduced to the Congress in 1923, and played an integral role in the reintroduction of the legislation in 1982. The organization has contributed over a million dollars toward passage of the ERA. It also has been supportive, financially and ideologically, of other forms of legislation aimed at equal rights, such as the Civil Rights Act of 1964, the Equal Pay Act, and Title IX of the Higher Education Act.[4]

This national organization has also started a number of programs recognizing and supporting women in the workplace. In 1928 it created National Business Women's Week and the Young Career Woman Program. Later came an educational foundation, a council on the women's future in the workplace, and a political action committee supporting "men and women candidates who share a commitment to total equality."[5] This organization develops a legislative platform each year. The 1986–87 platform statement appeared as follows:

> Because the fundamental law of the land is embodied in the Constitution of the United States and all statutory rights are derived therefrom, the Equal Rights Amendment shall stand first, foremost above all other items which may appear on the Legislative Platform of this Federation until equal legal rights for women and men become guaranteed in the U.S. Constitution.
> 1. Secure equal treatment for women in all areas of employment and support implementation of pay equity.
> 2. Reform laws governing Social Security and pension programs to achieve equity and adequacy for women.
> 3. Bring about equal treatment of women and men, regardless of marital status, in all phases of economic life, with special emphasis on the elimination of discrimination in insurance.
> 4. Support reproductive freedom as a right for all women.
> 5. Support equal educational opportunity at all levels.[6]

Within the last decade the national organization has had approximately 140,000 members and 3,500 clubs across the country. One of its local chapters formed the subject of this study. This chapter was founded in 1949 with 14 members and had grown to a membership of approximately 150 by 1988. While adhering to the national organization's platform, it has also developed unique programs. The chapter has worked to enact laws against drunk driving and domestic violence as well as, most recently, a state equal rights amendment (which failed by a narrow margin). Perhaps the best summary of the chapter's range of activities, as well as the various functions it performs to operate as an organization, can be provided through examination of the organization's structure and operating procedures.

STRUCTURE AND OPERATING PROCEDURES

This local business women's chapter is governed by a board of directors comprised of the executive officers representing eight elective offices and sixteen appointive committee chairs. Elective offices include a president, first vice-president, second vice-president, recording secretary, corresponding secretary, treasurer, parliamentarian, and auditor. A first vice-president oversees the committee system, which includes the bulletin (newsletter), Business Women's Week (plans events), by-laws (vehicle for proposing new amendments), civic affairs (community welfare activities), finance (prepares budget and oversees expenditures), foundation (participates in the funding of national scholarships), hospitality (arranges meeting places and dinner reservations), legislation (works to support the national platform), membership, mentoring (trains high school and college students in interviewing and résumé writing), personal advancement (career/leadership development), program (obtains speakers and programs for meetings), public relations, special events, yearbook, and young careerist (recognizes young women for their contribution to their profession and community). A second vice-president oversees and works with membership. The full board meets once a month to discuss major policy directions for the organization. The executive council sometimes meets more frequently. The entire local chapter holds business meetings once a month, on Wednesday nights from 5:30 to approximately 9:00 P.M.[7] Members, who pay yearly dues of $40, must make reservations in advance, as meetings are conducted over dinner. The meeting place rotates among a number of local hotels and restaurants. Generally, a cocktail/social hour is held between 5:30 and 6:00 P.M., and dinner is served between 6:00 and 7:00 P.M. while the president and the officers conduct the business meeting. This format is said to be useful because women can meet right after work rather than going home and coming back. Conducting business over dinner also has the benefit of saving time and providing business for a range of local establishments. The cost of the dinner varies between $10 and $12 per person. Approximately 40 percent of the membership attended meetings regularly during the period in which this organization was observed.

The business meeting is conducted formally, although it goes on while dinner is served.[8] Before everyone is seated there is a salute to the flag and an oath recited by all members. The president calls the meeting to order and the officer reports are delivered. If there are items on the agenda to be voted on, the membership votes based on majority rule. Any members wishing to speak out on an issue must get up and use a microphone at either end of the room. Officers have their own microphones at the head table, where all elective officers sit during the entire evening.

The members of the organization range in age from those just starting careers in their early twenties to those already retired. The average age is thirty-nine, considerably younger than the national average of fifty-nine. Occupationally, the greatest number of members (twenty-seven) are in financial careers such as accounting or banking. Business owners comprise the next largest category (eleven), followed closely by managers (ten), administrators (eight), and educators (seven). The remaining categories include insurance, general sales, computer industries, lawyers, marketing/advertising/media, and approximately fifteen retired members who were employed in the above categories, many of whom are former state and local chapter officers. This is a nonprofit, nonpartisan organization, although it does claim a political agenda. While the oath recited at every meeting makes a reference to God, no particular religious faith is observed by the organization.

ANALYSIS

Before considering data collected from interviews with the organization's members, it is important to recognize that the business women's group differs significantly from the two other groups in this study. First, it is considerably larger in membership than the other two organizations. The business group's "working core" or "active" group numbers thirty to forty, while that of the peace group and the health collective numbers approximately fifteen. As in the other two groups, the real work is done in committee or project groups. However, the way such small group meetings are conducted in the business group is different for there is very little evidence of consensual process. The purpose of each committee is generally dictated by the by-laws as described above. Where any flexibility exists, the board determines the specifics of committee activities. As one woman explains:

Unfortunately, when you are run by a board, what you can accomplish is determined by the board. Either you are an integral part of that, or you are sitting out there with your friends and not being too involved.

An example of this control would be the board's determination of whether, and in what way, the civic affairs committee will work with the local public TV station's fund-raising project. Additional evidence of this control from the top surfaces in comments from members who indicate that committee heads are not "tuned in" to the interests and ideas of the committee members. As another woman explains, "Committee chairs are not really listening to what the group wants to do and figuring out how to accomplish that." Some members said they had lost interest in participating as a result.

Of the fifteen women interviewed, none mentioned organizational structure, relative to feminist goals, as an issue. Their responses differed significantly from those of the women in the other two organizations studied. When asked why they joined the business women's group, most of the respondents claimed that they were looking for support from other women in the professions and opportunities to further their careers through networking with other women.

These responses, along with observation of meetings and research into organizational history, suggest a liberal feminist ideology as defined earlier in this research. It is important to note that some liberal feminist organizations are more concerned with questions of structure than others. Some, while accepting a degree of hierarchy, continually strive to minimize it.[9] While the business women's group is a participatory hierarchy, structure does not appear to be an issue. What becomes interesting in an analysis of this group is the relationship between the values of these women and the direction pursued by the organization to which they belong.

Hierarchy

The recognition of differences in both the size and operation of the business group leads immediately to a discussion of hierarchy. Responses to questions of who has power or who runs the organization reveal that both a formal and informal hierarchy exist.

Formal Hierarchy. The formal hierarchy is described above in the by-laws and formal operating procedures. Observation of meetings, as well as interviews with women in the group, provided evidence that this organization operated as a formal hierarchy. As a recent president of the group states, "The board is definitely the leadership, does a lot of preliminary work, and makes a lot of preliminary decisions which are usually accepted." The current president of the organization has the following to say about the relationship of the board to the rest of the organization:

> There has to be a head to keep order at meetings, but we get comments that people would like to mingle more with the board. The committee system is designed to keep members in touch with the board and get people involved and active with the organization. We give everybody the opportunity to pick a committee to be on, and I guess people don't want to work on committees. Very few send in interest forms, so the president picks the committee chairs and the first vice-president fills the committees. You might assign ten people and get two to three.

Yet another member says the following about the operation of the organization: "A lot of ideas come from the board and a lot of members are willing to have it that way." Yet another member confirms the role of the board and committee heads as follows: "The board determines overall direction of the group. The president and vice-presidents set goals. Committee chairs have some discretion, but it has to be approved by the board."

Of the fifteen women interviewed, nearly all focused on the role of the board in running their organization. Those who did not focused on an informal hierarchy.

Informal Hierarchy. The informal hierarchy within the business women's group is comprised of retired women of long standing within the organization as well as experience in its elective offices. Many older members (generally defined as those who have retired from their professions) say they are ignored by younger members, but this is not entirely true. In the two years in which this organization was studied, older members did not hold key elective posts, yet this did not exclude these members from key decision making. Older members who had also served as local presidents or state officers comprised an informal hierarchy. A few of them held committee posts and therefore would occasionally appear at board meetings. Members of the informal hierarchy influenced decision making by exerting pressure on newer, younger officers and members to conduct the business of the organization "by the book," or as dictated by the national organization.

Older members who were not former presidents or key office holders in the organization were in a very real sense ignored. These members felt that they did not participate in decision making and that the organization did not address their needs. This concern is illustrated by the comments of the following thirty-year member:

> I think the officers run the club, the executive board. I would like to see more involvement with the membership body. When it comes to finances, members should be more involved. Dues, dinners, and requests for other contributions get to be too much. But also I'd like to mix more with the younger people. It would be nice to get to know the officers better, but they don't seem to have the time or the interest. I do think the organization as a whole discriminates against the older members. They say we can't hold offices and do certain things. I don't think the organization should discriminate against anyone.

This statement is representative of the view of older members who appear to have little influence on the organization as a whole. Those falling into this category slightly outnumber those with influence. Those with influence are described by younger members as quite controlling and constantly complaining. An example of their complaints is as follows:

> The meetings are more relaxed now. When I was first in the organization, everything was by *Robert's Rules*. They don't pay much attention to that now. They move through business very quickly over dinner, and I'm not sure I like that.

When young members, particularly officers, are asked questions concerning who holds power in the organization, they point to the group of former officers mentioned above. Perhaps most surprising was the response of a woman who had been a member of the organization for less than a year. When she was asked who ran the organization, she simply responded: "The older members control it." Other comments from young members indicate feelings of pressure from what some call the "old guard." For example, a newly elected president had this to say:

> I want to do things right and I don't want to make any mistakes, but I know that I will. There are some older members, one in particular, who [are] very critical. She sent me a congratulatory card when I became president, but if I make a mistake I know she'll be right on me.

Another example of how young members view the older former officers is provided by the words of the outgoing president:

When I first joined [six years ago] it seemed to me that everything was decided at the board level. The members had no impact whatsoever. There are a lot of traditional things about this organization that people don't want to change, and those people are not the younger board members; they are the older past presidents. These people don't want to make changes that would bring in younger, more active women. It is always, "when I was president we did it this way," and that makes it very tough. It makes people turn away from responsibility. New officers can't express themselves the way they want with the new ideas they have. They feel it is very structured, or if they do something wrong they are going to hear about it.

Other young members characterize the problem in these ways:

The organization is divided into cliques. The perception is that the older members are really powerful. If you don't do what they want you to, they can really cause problems for you personally.

The older group who have been members for a long time are so vocal about what they want that even the new people who take leadership positions end up not being able to do it. The old group is still there nitpicking and complaining. I really think we should split off into two groups.

Personal observation of meetings confirmed, at the very least, the "oversight" function of the older former presidents. For example, any new person at a meeting, this researcher included, was sought out by these older members and questioned carefully about her reasons for being there. While the questioning was not unfriendly, one received the sense that these members were taking note of everything that occurred at the meeting.

In addition, a member of this group would almost always speak out on issues raised in the formal meeting. This is significant, because there was not a great amount of discussion on business issues at any of the meetings observed over the two-year period. Decisions seemed already to have been made, the purpose of the meeting being to inform the rest of the membership of them. Younger members may have been deterred from speaking by nervousness about leaving their seat at a dinner table to cross the room to use the microphone. Some members did mention, in their interviews, being bothered by this procedure, whereas, older members did not mention it as a problem, nor did they seem to shy away from microphone use. Perhaps a function of their former leadership roles, this participation created a strong sense of their presence and activism.

To summarize on the subject of hierarchy within the business women's group, there appears to be a formal hierarchy of elected officers as designated by the formal rules of the organization, and an informal hierarchy of retired members who are former elected state and local officers. While many members believe that the board "runs" the organization through its hierarchy of officers and committee posts at various levels, they also acknowledge the influence of this older, informal group. It appears that the pressure exerted by the informal group to some extent offsets the formal powers of the elected officers. Because of this, decision making in the organization works more through compromise and accommodation than one would expect. The following analysis of major issues within the organization helps to clarify this point.

Conflicting Goals: The Networking Versus Civic Argument

A great deal of conflict within this organization stems from unclear or differing goals. Statements such as "The organization has lost its focus," "They don't know what it is they want to accomplish," or "The organization is too broad" reflect a problem with goals. When asked what the organization's goals are, members' responses tend to reflect a statement in their handbook: the goal is "women helping women." As the women discuss this goal, however, they reveal confusion around it. One younger woman responded in this way:

> The goal is women helping women, but where do you start? I think it is difficult to get an organization our size to have one focus. We have a range of different ages and interests and we don't have one focus like the Lion's Club. I think we need to refocus. We need stronger leadership and a way to bring this group together. We are too fragmented.

Another younger member describes the problem she sees:

> The sense I began to get from the organization, and the reason I am less involved, is that they don't really know what it is they do want to accomplish. There are very clear group factions within the organization and they don't have a clear goal. They don't know if they want to be social, a professional network, or an information network of speakers on certain topics.

Basically, the organization can be broken down into two groups: those interested in networking and those interested in civic activities. Evidence from interviews suggests that the service of civic orientation can be traced to former officers. One woman near retirement age described what she saw as a transition:

> Many years ago the club was more casual in the sense that the activities were more like those of a women's club, more civic-oriented. There was a formal part of the organization in that things were fairly well controlled by the national in terms of the activities we were suppose to do. Meetings were always conducted by *Robert's Rules of Order*. Somewhere in there we made the transition from a women's club to a professional club.

The woman speaking believes the transition from civic to professional organization to be complete. Other interviews show that this is not the case. For instance, consider these comments by a younger member:

> The older group sees themselves as a civic organization. Then there is a part of the group that sees themselves networking and improving themselves professionally. And maybe there is just a social group that could do just the civic things. I think a lot of frustration stems from the other people who don't want to pay their dues civically. They just want to use the group for a network. Maybe that is why the older group gets so upset—because we don't buy into the ritual or give a darn about the national. Those are the things you always hear: "The younger group doesn't support the public TV auction anymore," and a range of other things. If the civic group would do those things, then the networking group could network.

The Networking Group. This group of women is mainly interested in the ways in which this organization can help them with career advancement. They want the organization to provide programs and attract new members to give them information and connections. These women say they joined the organization primarily for business contacts: "to promote working women and set up a women's network." While these women fully support equal rights for women, they tend to accept the realities of male hierarchies: that they will be discriminated against and have to work harder because of it. The following statement reflects this point of view: "If you are going to be in business and do business, you have to gain respect on your own as an individual. Deal with the fact that you are definitely going to be treated unequally. That's a reality."

Their major criticism of the business women's group is that it does not help women to "do business." The following statement illustrates this point:

> I see business going on at a lot of the meetings of other [male] organizations. I did not see business going on at our meetings. I saw a lot of socializing going on. In other words, there were no dollars and cents deals. There were no handshake deals going on. I didn't see a lot of decision making going on or people taking responsibility for doing business with each other. All of my business mentors have been very successful men. Networking on a business level means doing business with other people who can help promote your career.

Part of the problem, from the standpoint of those who want to network, is that a large part of the business group's membership is drawn from mid-level rather than top-level positions. The kind of top-level network some members are looking for is not readily available. In other words, members are not in positions in which they might help someone coming up through the ranks. As one new member points out, "This organization is comprised of women who are not top managers. They are not the key decision makers in their places of work. My sense of it is that the real "power people" don't have time for this organization." Another woman explains it this way: "In the business women's group, women are new to their professions, trying to get their bearings. You don't get a sense that they are connected to the real political implications of the workplace."

The woman speaking in this next interview belongs to another group, made up of women business owners. She compares and contrasts the two groups, explaining that she gains much more from the business owners' group because it is more narrowly focused. It is not a civic group, but is organized to lend support and information to women attempting to run their own businesses. This particular woman, the publisher of a statewide feminist tabloid, talks about what she expects to gain from membership in the business women's group:

> I belong to a women business owners' group. There is an immediate bonding and respect. I, [like] the other women in the business owners' group, want to learn something at a meeting. If I have learned one thing, I'm happy. I'm not getting that out of the business women's group. The business owners' group has hit the real world: banking, getting loans, not getting into male business clubs. The business women's group hasn't connected with this yet. They gloss over the real issues.

These statements indicate that those who want to "network" think the group is not maximizing networking potential by attracting top-level people or providing information women need to make it to the top levels of their fields. Some of these members are becoming less active with the group. One characterizes the problem this way:

> What would be most important would be to do things that would attempt to attract the kinds of professionals we want to network with. And I think that is what has happened: With the types of speakers and the frustration of the meetings, the kinds of professionals you hope to network with have given up and don't attend anymore. We could still use a program format, but invite speakers who could be later used as professional contacts. We should be very open about that.

Part of the business women's group, then, wants to make networking the major goal of the organization. While some networking currently goes on, it is not perceived to have reached a level these women would consider valuable. Consequently, they are pulling away from the organization.

The Civic Group. At the other end of the spectrum are women who want to broaden the organization's scope to draw in all working women rather than simply professional women. These are members who said in their interviews, "This organization is for all working women and we have to do more to bring these women in."

These women realize how far they have come in their careers and want to extend what they have learned to others, especially those just starting out or reentering the work force. They want to bring in clerical workers, nurses, and women who tend not to define themselves as "professionals." This aspect of the organization's goals is evidenced by civic programs such as mentoring and fund-raising projects.

In general, the civic aspect of the organization tends to be supported by the older members. They talk about the support the organization lends to women in the workplace. This is very different from the concept of networking described by the younger women of the organization. The concept of support concerns sharing the problems that face working women, rather than the idea of "getting ahead," which is characteristic of networking. For instance, one older member responded this way when asked why she joined the organization:

> It was one of the few organizations for working women at the time and it was good to have the support of the group. . . . The reason

I joined was to have contacts with other businesspeople and along with that the sociability and getting to know people and broadening of my knowledge of other businesses.

While other older members interviewed indicated similar reasons for joining the organization, they were not the only members holding this support/civic view. There are some younger members who also support the more civic goals and are not as centered on networking as other younger members. One younger woman who has been in the organization for six years said: "I joined to meet other businesswomen and also to get involved in some worthwhile projects." One younger woman, who had just been elected president, expressed this view with regard to networking and civic balance in the organization:

> The reason people come is because of networking. I do believe there is more to this organization than networking. There are a lot of women out there in the community who need our help: single heads of households, students, battered women to name a few. This goes beyond networking. We need to do something for all types of working women. Sometimes we get a little snobby about it. Our challenge is to attract women from other jobs, but there are problems with that, not the least of which is money. It costs $40 a year to belong to this organization and $12 a month to come to meetings. Some of the women I would like to attract can't afford that.

The evidence suggests that not only the older group but also some younger members support civic goals within this organization. Yet the tendency among the younger women interested in networking is to associate the civic aspects of the organization with older members. Since older members were often the first women to enter certain jobs in their fields, it is easy to see why they view the support aspect of the group as so important. The younger members may not need support in the same way that the older members did, because they have not necessarily been the first women in their areas of work. This is why the concept of getting ahead through networking may be of more importance to them.

Whatever the reasons for these differences among members concerning the goals of the organization, the goals do lead in different directions. One path broadens the base of the organization by bringing in more representatives of mid-level occupations, while the other path offers access to women who have achieved the top levels of their professions. At the time of study, the organization had taken no major step to move in either direction. It simply continued on a middle-of-the-road path, which has led to a decline in membership.

Female- Versus Male-Related Values. The fact that these women tend
to be mid-level in their careers is symbolic of women's struggle with
different values and the point at which many women had arrived in
the late 1980s. The different values are thought to be female- and
male-related values.

Male-related values—those linked to hierarchy—are reflected by
the women who emphasize networking and getting to the next level
in their careers. They very rightly recognize that they work in male-
run hierarchies, that they are at a disadvantage in that marketplace,
and that this success will come through their own personal hard work
and conviction. They believe that their personal success will do more
to advance women as a group than any range of civic or legislative
programs. As they move up the ladder in their professions, the network will help those below them to improve their positions.

Women representing the civic-oriented perspective look to develop
an organization that is supportive in a collective sense. While their
liberal feminism does not lead them to challenge the organization's
hierarchical structure, their interest in extending the membership to
encompass other professions and women in need reflects female-re-
lated values.

To a great extent, all members of the organization, as individuals,
are torn over the conflict between a civic and a networking focus.
Some attempt to balance these views, while others do not. As a whole,
the organization attempts to maintain balance and accommodate the
conflict over values. In doing this, it pays a price. The price is constant
conflict, frustration, and a declining membership.

NOTES

1. Business group *Yearbook*, 1986–1987, p. 17.
2. Ibid.
3. Ibid.
4. Ibid., p. 18.
5. Business Women's Association brochure (printed by the national organization.)
6. *Yearbook*, p. 18.
7. Please note that the description of meetings with regard to specifics of time,
and the use of time at meetings, refers to the period in which this study was conducted.
8. This procedure was later changed so that the business meeting would begin
after dinner. The change was made to allow members the chance to socialize during dinner.
9. See Robin Leidner, "Stretching the Boundaries of Liberalism: Democratic
Innovation in a Feminist Organization," *Signs* 16, no. 2 (1991).

EIGHT

Summary and Conclusion

Three feminist organizations, two anarchist and one liberal, have been observed. Findings are that the anarchist feminist groups were able, during the two-year period of observation and interviewing, to maintain non-hierarchical organization while at the same time achieving, to a reasonable extent, organization goals. The liberal feminist group, as expected, maintained a hierarchical organization. As explained earlier, for liberal feminists, development of non-hierarchical organization is not an immediate goal. However, as argued in the chapter describing this group, a great deal of conflict existed among organization members over goals. Values behind these goals were related to the hierarchy/non-hierarchy argument, with a networking group willing to work through hierarchy for the advancement of women, and the civic group wanting to help women in supportive/community-oriented ways.

Because the two anarchist groups have as a stated goal the building of non-hierarchical organization, they have been the most important to this study. Further, of these two organizations, the health collective clearly provides the most important data because of the constraints under which it operates as a business rather than a volunteer organization. As discussed earlier, the health collective must maintain its business financially and provide quality health care to women as well as maintain the political goals of providing an example of non-hierarchical structure. In this way, the health collective must contend with a number of business, legal, and ethical constraints that many volunteer organizations never face.

Given these differences in the two organizations, it is significant that their structure is remarkably similar.[1] As indicated, both organizations explicitly state that they are committed to building and maintaining non-hierarchical organization. Commitment to this goal has led both organizations in the same direction. This has been aided by the fact that both groups have the same number of active members (approximately fifteen), and have not had to contend with the problem of factions to the same extent as larger organizations such as the business group.

MODIFIED CONSENSUS

Uniqueness of the Structure

One of the most significant aspects of these organizations, and the most important finding of this study, is the structure that flows from the particular way in which these women seem to make decisions. First, they are keenly aware of a distinction between critical and routine decisions. As stated in the health collective chapter, decisions that are critical are those that have the potential to change the organization's direction. Those that are routine are important to its daily operation but not likely to raise significant questions about overall policy. Within the literature on organizations, the distinction between critical and routine decisions is not new. What is new is the way in which feminists have structured organizations in light of this distinction.

In both the health collective and the peace group, critical decisions are reserved for the entire membership, while routine decisions are delegated horizontally. For example, in the peace group, project groups make routine decisions. In the health collective, the coordinators and their respective committees make such decisions. It is recognized that routine decisions have the potential to become critical. In the event that they do, they are reconsidered by the entire group.

What is unique about the structure of these anarchist groups is that everyone is involved in making critical policy. In hierarchical organizations, only those at the top make critical policy, with varying degrees of input from lower levels. In the anarchist groups, routine decisions also are delegated horizontally to those who have an interest in making them. While such delegation can involve additional responsibility, authority, and expertise, it does not result in a superordinate/subordinate relationship.

In the peace group, some rotation of members through tasks helps to ensure that hierarchy does not develop. Because it is a volunteer organization, it can afford the organizational costs involved in retraining members in new areas. The health collective decided that it could not afford these costs and therefore relied on the process of the organization, including trust among members, to avoid development of hierarchy.

Thus, while the most important defining element of these structures is the reservation of critical decisions for the entire membership and the delegation of routine decisions to the few, other aspects of the internal environment are important to maintaining non-hierarchical structure. These aspects are best described by the term *process*, which includes the concepts of consensus, empowerment, and emerging leadership as discussed in previous chapters. Without trust among members fostered through consensus decision making and a conscious effort to avoid domination, hierarchy would be difficult to avoid. In this way, the political ideals of the members, the ideological commitments to non-hierarchy, are vitally important.

Through study of these anarchist groups, a model of modified consensual organization has been constructed. Again, the most important defining element is the delegation of routine decisions to the few and the reservation of critical decisions for the many. An example of such delegation in the peace group is the group's representative to the Peace and Justice Center's board. This person has an awareness of which decisions are critical and should be brought back to the organization as a whole. This person once was asked to approve a new group's entry to center membership. The group seeking to enter the center was not committed to nonviolence. The admission of a group not committed to nonviolence could have had great impact on all the center organizations. The peace group's representative to the Peace and Justice Center recognized this as a critical decision, one her entire organization would need to discuss. This type of decision is carried back to the full membership.

Operating Mechanisms

For the peace group and health collective alike, recognition of ability or expertise within their memberships is important. The structure of the peace group, including its project groups, Redirection and Community Action, maximizes the skills of its membership. It also has an educational function, in that those who wish to work in an area they know little about may rotate into that area and be trained by other members. Rotation allows for personal development. For the health collective, rotation of tasks has become more difficult, because of the costs of retraining. Some tasks within the clinic and administrative jobs at the front desk rotate, while other tasks have developed into permanent positions.

This structure developed out of ten years of experimentation in finding the best ways to recognize and utilize expertise within the organization, and led to development of the coordinator positions. Coordinators are delegated responsibility from the entire staff/board. Yet they also have a responsibility to educate the rest of the staff as to their knowledge of a specific area of routine work, such as medical protocol.

Another characteristic of this modified non-hierarchical structure is an attempt to minimize power and maximize empowerment. For women in both the peace group and health collective, power is described as something bestowed upon a person or something that is taken from someone else. It is a relational concept that has a win/lose element to it. For the women of the peace group and health collective, voting as a form of decision making is perceived as a win/lose situation. That is why they reject voting as a main form of decision making. Voting, for these women, means that there will always be some organization members who perceive they have "lost." With consensus decision making, based on the concept of empowerment, it is perceived that everyone "wins" because all members agree to the final decision. In this way, empowerment is a key concept behind the operation of the group. It relates to the structure and, in the attempt to avoid positions and rank, to the organization's operation through consensus.

A third characteristic of this model is clarity of goals. It is interesting that descriptions and discussions centering on consensual organization often indicate that goals are diffuse. This was a criticism of the consciousness-raising groups of the women's movement in the 1960s and '70s. For these groups, this criticism may have been valid. But it does not apply to the peace group or to the health collective. Goals for both these groups are very clear. In the case of the health collective, the goal is providing quality health care for and by women, in the context of feminist goals of equality for women. The peace group's goals are to work for peace and justice as a group committed to feminist goals, with a specific focus on working against the manufacture and sale of war toys. The women interviewed in both these organizations were able to state these goals and explain how their organization worked toward them.

Members of these groups also indicated that as the structure of the organization evolved, goals became clearer. In addition, they believed that a relationship existed between clear goals and the ease with which consensual process could work. They explained that clarity of goals led to a foundation upon which consensus could be built. Goals often reflect values held by an organization's members. If there is a similarity in values, consensus is possible, because there is little divisive opinion. Thus, clarity of goals becomes an important element in a non-hierarchical model. It is interesting to note that the leading complaint of women in the business group was confusion over goals. In this case, conflicting goals became associated with hierarchical, non-consensual structure.

There was a great degree of conflict over what the business group's organizational goals should be and how their organization should work to achieve those goals, once identified. The "networking" group wanted to utilize membership connections in a way that was very concrete, by actually entering into business dealings with other members. The "civic" group indicated an interest in the general social support of other women in the professions. The stated goals of the organization indicated both these interests. The result was very real conflict within the organization.

Given the above discussion, modified consensual organization may be seen to contain the following components: a distinction between critical and routine decisions, with critical decisions reserved for the many and routine decisions delegated horizontally to the few; recognition of ability or expertise rather than rank or position; empowerment as a basis of consensual process; and clear goals arrived at through consensual process.

TOWARD DECISIONS WITHOUT HIERARCHY

The subject of decisions without hierarchy has never received more public attention than it is receiving now. A vast array of organizations, from computer firms to universities to auto makers, are currently attempting to restructure at least part of their decision-making processes in order to become more consensual. The question is: Why? At least part of the answer lies in the fact that women who have had experience with consensus, and prefer it to voting and hierarchy, have brought the idea into the workplace. As more and more of these women have achieved positions of decision making within large-scale organizations, they have been able to implement their ideas. This is the result of feminist interventions.

Interestingly, at the same time, Japanese firms operating by consensus have made their way into the United States and demonstrated that consensual structure can produce high-quality products and high-level sales. One need only look at the success of Honda and Toyota to substantiate this point. By comparison, the hierarchically organized American autofirms have been left in the dust. With record low sales, some are now making attempts at emulating Japanese firms.[2] In this and other cases, prospects for profit have brought intense attention to the benefits of consensus, which feminists and others have known about for decades.

As corporate leaders have assessed both the positive and negative aspects of hierarchy, they have come to recognize the importance of small group behavior within a larger decision-making process. They have accepted the curvilinear relationship between information-processing requirements and the utility of hierarchy: hierarchy is not efficient in organizational settings where there is too little *or* too much information. At the very least they are asking the question: To what extent can the consensual process exhibited by some small groups be applied in large-scale organization settings?

This study contributes to the literature of organizations with regard to the above question. The modified consensual structure developed by the health collective in particular distinguishes decision-making types in a way that needs to be tested in large-scale organizations. Critical decisions reserved for the many and routine decisions delegated horizontally to the few circumvent some major problems for which consensual-style organization has been criticized.

While consensual organizations focus less on efficiency as an important goal, constraints in the environment of large-scale organizations make efficiency difficult to ignore. The distinction between critical and routine decisions as implemented by the health collective responds to a need for efficiency with regard to routine matters. This kind of structure may provide enough efficiency for some types of larger-scale organizations, particularly high-technology industries.[3]

It is sometimes difficult in a world that operates by hierarchy to find the language to describe another mode of operation. The identification and description of the modified consensual model of the anarchist feminist organizations that are the focus of this study represents an attempt to do this. The development of this model is only a beginning, not an end. The pervasiveness of this type of organization needs to be documented. The question of gender differences in organizations needs to be explored. By addressing these new questions, we will expand the range of possible structures, from which we may select those best suited to achieve organization goals.

NOTES

1. There is no overlapping membership between the groups.
2. See General Motors' new Saturn plant, for example.
3. William G. Ouchi, "Markets, Bureaucracies, and Clans," *Administrative Science Quarterly* 225 (March 1980): 129–41.

BIBLIOGRAPHY

BOOKS ON HIERARCHY, IDEOLOGY, AND ORGANIZATIONS

Argyris, Chris. *Interpersonal Competence and Organizational Effectiveness.* Homewood, Ill.: Dorsey, 1962.
———. *Personality and Organization.* New York: Harper & Row, 1957.
Barnard, Chester I. *The Functions of the Executive.* Cambridge, Mass.: Harvard University Press, 1938.
Bennis, Warren G. *American Bureaucracy.* Chicago: Aldine, 1970.
Blau, Peter. *The Dynamics of Bureaucracy.* Chicago: University of Chicago Press, 1963.
Blau, Peter, and W. Richard Scott. *Formal Organizations.* San Francisco: Chandler, 1962.
Dahl, Robert. *After the Revolution? Authority in a Good Society.* New Haven: Yale University Press, 1970.
Downs, Anthony. *Inside Bureaucracy.* Waltham, Mass.: Little, Brown, 1968.
Duverger, Maurice. *Political Parties.* London: Methuen, 1954.
Elazar, Daniel J. *American Federalism: A View From the States.* New York: Crowell, 1972.
Freeman, Jo. *The Politics of Women's Liberation.* New York: Longman, 1975.

Hummel, Ralph P. *The Bureaucratic Experience.* New York: St. Martin's, 1977.

Kaufman, Herbert. *The Forest Ranger.* Baltimore: Johns Hopkins University Press, 1967.

Ladd, Carl Everett. *Ideology In America.* Ithaca: Cornell University Press, 1969.

Likert, Rensis. *New Patterns of Management.* New York: McGraw-Hill, 1961.

Lindblom, Charles. *Politics and Markets.* New York: Basic Books, 1977.

Lipset, Seymour Martin, and James S. Coleman. *Union Democracy.* Glencoe, Ill.: The Free Press, 1956.

Lowi, Theodore J. *The Politics of Disorder.* New York: Basic Books, 1971.

Mannheim, Karl. *Ideology and Utopia.* New York: Harcourt, Brace & Co., 1954.

———. *Man and Society.* New York: Harcourt, Brace & Co., 1940.

McGregor, Douglas. *The Human Side of Enterprise.* New York: McGraw-Hill, 1960.

Meyer, Marshall W., and Associates, ed. *Environments and Organizations.* San Francisco: Jossey-Bass, 1978.

Michels, Robert. *Political Parties.* New York: The Free Press, 1962.

Mooney, James D. *The Principles of Organization.* New York: Harper & Bros., 1947.

Ott, Steven J. *The Organization Culture Perspective.* Pacific Grove: Brooks/Cole, 1989.

Pigors, Paul. *Leadership or Domination.* London: George C. Harrap & Co., 1935.

Presthus, Robert. *The Organizational Society.* New York: Vintage, 1965.

Safire, William. *Safire's Political Dictionary.* New York: Ballantine, 1978.

Salaman, Graeme, and Kenneth Thompson, eds. *Control and Ideology in Organizations.* Cambridge, Mass.: MIT Press, 1980.

Schuman, David. *The Ideology of Form.* Lexington, Mass.: D. C. Heath, 1978.

Scott, W. Richard. *Organizations.* Englewood Cliffs, N.J.: Prentice-Hall, 1981.

Scruton, Roger. *A Dictionary of Political Thought.* New York: Harper & Row, 1982.

Selznick, Philip. *Leadership in Administration.* New York: Harper & Row, 1957.

Sennett, Richard. *Authority.* New York: Alfred A. Knopf, 1980.

———. *The Fall of Public Man.* New York: Vintage, 1978.

Simon, Herbert A. *The Shape of Automation for Men and Management.* New York: Harper & Row, 1965.

Spence, Larry. *The Politics of Social Knowledge.* University Park, Pa.: Pennsylvania State University Press, 1978.

Tannenbaum, Arnold S., and B. Kavcic, M. Rosner, M. Vianello, and G. Wiesner. *Hierarchy in Organizations: An International Comparison.* San Francisco: Jossey-Bass, 1974.

Thompson, Victor. *Modern Organizations.* New York: Alfred A. Knopf, 1965.

Weber, Max. *The Theory of Social and Economic Organizations,* ed. A. M. Henderson and Talcott Parsons. New York: The Free Press, 1964.

Yates, Douglas. *Bureaucratic Democracy.* Cambridge, Mass.: Harvard University Press, 1982.

Zald, Mayer N. *Power in Organizations.* Nashville: Vanderbilt University Press, 1970.

Zey-Ferrell, Mary, and Michael Aiken, eds. *Complex Organizations: Critical Perspectives.* Glenview, Ill.: Scott, Foresman & Co., 1981.

ARTICLES ON HIERARCHY, IDEOLOGY, AND ORGANIZATIONS

Benson, J. Kenneth. "Organizations: A Dialectical View," in Zey-Ferrell and Aiken.

Cassinelli, C. W. "The Law of Oligarchy," *American Political Science Review* 47 (1953):773–84.

Denhardt, Robert B., and Jan Perkins. "The Coming Death of Administrative Man," *Women in Administration* 36 (July/Aug. 1976):382.

Goldman, Paul, and Donald R. Van Houten. "Bureaucracy and Domination: Managerial Strategy in Turn-of-the-Century American Industry," in Zey-Ferrell and Aiken.

McNeil, Kenneth. "Understanding Organizational Power: Building on the Weberian Legacy," in Zey-Ferrell and Aiken.

Merton, Robert K. "Bureaucratic Structure and Personality," in R. Merton, *Social Theory and Social Structure* (New York: The Free Press, 1968).

Ouchi, William, and Alfred M. Jaeger. "Type Z Organization: Stability in the Modst of Mobility," *Academy of Management Review* 3 (April 1978).

Ouchi, William, and Jerry Johnson. "Types of Organization Control and Their Relationship to Emotional Well-Being," *Administrative Science Quarterly* 23 (June 1978).

Ouchi, William G. "Markets, Bureaucracies and Clans," *Administrative Science Quarterly* 225 (March 1980).

Pelz, Donald C. "Leadership Within a Hierarchical Organization," *Journal of Social Issues* 7 (1951):49–55.

Shils, Edward. "Ideology: The Concept and Function of Ideology," in the *International Encyclopedia of Social Sciences* (New York: Macmillan, 1930).

Spence, Larry. "Prolegomena to a Communications Theory of Human Organizations," unpublished manuscript (Department of Political Science, University of California, Berkeley, Jan. 1969.)

FEMINIST BOOKS

Boneparth, Ellen. *Women, Power & Policy.* New York: Pergamon, 1982.

Bunch, Charlotte. *Building Feminist Theory: Essays from Quest.* New York: Longman, 1981.

Deckard, Barbara Sinclair. *The Women's Movement.* New York: Harper & Row, 1979.

Donovan, Josephine. *Feminist Theory.* New York: Ungar, 1986.

Eisenstein, Hester. *Gender Shock.* Boston: Beacon, 1991.

Eisenstein, Zillah R. *Capitalist Patriarchy and the Case for Socialist Feminism.* New York: Monthly Review Press, 1979.

———. *The Radical Future of Liberal Feminism.* New York: Longman, 1981.

Elshtain, Jean B. *Public Man/Private Woman: Women in Social and Political Thought.* Princeton: Princeton University Press, 1981.

Evans, Sara. *Personal Politics.* New York: Alfred A. Knopf, 1979.

Ferguson, Kathy. *The Feminist Case Against Bureaucracy.* Philadelphia: Temple University Press, 1984.

———. *Self, Society and Womankind: The Dialectic of Liberation.* Westbury, Conn.: Greenwood Press, 1980.

Figes, Eva. *Patriarchal Attitudes.* Greenwich, Conn.: Fawcett, 1970.

Firestone, Shulamith. *The Dialectic of Sex.* New York: Morrow, 1970.

Flexnor, Eleanor. *Century of Struggle.* Cambridge, Mass.: Harvard University Press, 1966.

French, Marilyn. *Beyond Power.* New York: Summit, 1985.

Friedan, Betty. *The Feminine Mystique.* London: Victor Gollancz, 1963.

Gilligan, Carol. *In A Different Voice.* Cambridge, Mass.: Harvard University Press, 1982.

Hartsock, Nancy. *Money, Sex, and Power: Toward a Feminist Historical Materialism.* New York: Longman, 1983.

Hiller, Dana V., and Robin Ann Sheets. *Women & Men: The Consequences of Power.* Cincinnati: University of Cincinnati, 1976.

Kanter, Rosabeth Moss. *Men and Women of the Corporation.* New York: Basic Books, 1977.

Love, Nancy. *Dogmas and Dreams.* Chatham, N.J.: Chatham House Publishers, 1991.

Mansbridge, Jane J. *Why We Lost the ERA.* Chicago: University of Chicago Press, 1986.

Millett, Kate. *Sexual Politics.* New York: Doubleday, 1970.

Millman, Marcia, and Rosabeth Moss Kanter. *Another Voice.* New York: Doubleday, 1975.

Morgan, Robin. *Sisterhood is Global.* New York: Anchor, 1984.

Sanday, Peggy Reeves. *Female Power and Male Dominance.* New York: Cambridge University Press, 1981.

Sargent, Lydia. *Women and Revolution.* Boston: South End, 1981.

Stacey, Margaret, and Marion Price. *Women, Power and Politics*. London: Tavistock, 1981.
Tong, Rosemarie. *Feminist Thought*. Boulder: Westview, 1989.

FEMINIST ARTICLES

Bunch, Charlotte. "Feminism and Politics," *Boston Mobilizer*, March/April, 1981.
Carroll, Berenice A. "Political Science, Part I: American Politics and Political Behavior," *Signs* 5, no. 2 (Winter 1979).
Ehrlich, Carol. "An Anarchafeminist Looks at Power Relationships," *Quest* 5, no. 4
Freeman, Jo. "The Tyranny of Structurelessness," in Jane Jaquette, ed. *Women in Politics*. New York: Wiley, 1974.
Freeman, Jo. "The Women's Liberation Movement: Its Origins, Organizations, Activities, and Ideas," in Jo Freeman, ed. *Women: A Feminist Perspective* (Palo Alto: Mayfield, 1979.)
Gordon, Suzanne. "The New Corporate Feminism," *The Nation* 236 (February 5, 1983): 129–47.
Hartsock, Nancy. "Political Change: Two Perspectives on Power," *Quest: A Feminist Quarterly* 1 (Summer 1974).
Hartsock, Nancy. "Foucault on Power: A Theory for Women?" in Linda Nicholson, ed. *Feminism/Postmodernism* (New York: Routledge, 1990.)
Hole, Judith, and Ellen Levine. "The First Feminists," in Freeman, *Women: A Feminist Perspective* (Palo Alto: Mayfield, 1979.)
Leidner, Robin. "Stretching the Boundaries of Liberalism: Democratic Innovation in a Feminist Organization," *Signs* 16, no. 2 (1991).
Martin, Patricia Yancey. "Rethinking Feminist Organizations," *Gender and Society* 4, no. 2 (June 1990).
Ruddick, Sara. "Maternal Thinking," *Feminist Studies* 6 (Summer 1980): pp. 342–67.
Sacks, Karen. "Networking: When Potluck is Political," *Ms.*, April 1983, pp. 97–98.

BOOKS ON POWER

Bachrach, Samuel B., and Edward J. Lawler. *Power and Politics in Organizations*. London: Jossey-Bass, 1980.
Bachrach, Peter, and Morton S. Baratz. *Power & Poverty*. New York: Oxford University Press, 1970.
Bell, David V. *Power, Influence, and Authority*. New York: Oxford University Press, 1975.

Dahl, Robert. *A Preface to Democratic Theory.* Chicago: University of Chicago Press, 1956.

Domhoff, G. William. *Who Rules America?* Englewood Cliffs, N.J.: Prentice-Hall, 1967.

Duverger, Maurice. *The Idea of Politics.* Chicago: Henry Regnery, 1970.

Hunter, Floyd. *Community Power Succession: Atlanta's Policy Makers Revisited.* Chapel Hill: University of North Carolina Press, 1980.

Katznelson, Ira, and Mark Kesselman. *The Politics of Power.* New York: Harcourt Brace Jovanovich, 1975.

Kipnis, David. *The Powerholders.* Chicago: University of Chicago Press, 1976.

Lukes, Stephen. *Power: A Radical View.* London: Macmillan, 1974.

McConnell, Grant. *Private Power and American Democracy.* New York: Vintage, 1970.

Moore, Barrington. *Political Power and Social Theory, Seven Studies.* New York: Harper & Row, 1965.

Russell, Bertrand. *Power: A New Social Analysis.* New York Norton, 1938.

ARTICLES ON POWER

Bachrach, Peter, and Morton Baratz. "The Two Faces of Power," *American Political Science Review* 56 (1962).

Carroll, Berenice. "Peace Research: The Cult of Power" (paper read at the annual convention of the American Sociological Association, Denver, Colorado, Sept. 1, 1971).

Cartwright, Dorwin. "Influence, Leadership, Control," in J. G. March, ed., *Handbook of Organizations* (Chicago: Rand-McNally, 1965), pp. 1–47.

Dahl, Robert A. "The Concept of Power," *Behavioral Science 2* (1957): 201–18.

Emerson, R. M. "Power-Dependence Relations," *American Sociological Review* 27 (1962): 31–41.

French, John R. P., and Bertram Raven. "The Basis of Social Power," in Darwin Cartwright, ed., *Studies in Social Power* (Ann Arbor: University of Michigan, Institute for Social Research, 1959), pp. 150–67.

Raven, Bertram H. "The Comparative Analysis of Power and Influence," in J. T. Tedeschi, ed., *Perspectives on Social Power* (Chicago: Aldine, 1974).

BOOKS ON SMALL GROUPS AND CONSENSUAL ORGANIZATION

Bennis, Warren G. *Beyond Bureaucracy: Essays on the Development and Evolution of Human Organization.* New York: McGraw-Hill, 1966.

Gerlach, Luther P., and Virginia H. Hine. *People, Power, Change: Movements of Social Transformation.* Indianapolis: Bobbs-Merrill, 1970.

Greenberg, Edward S. *Workplace Democracy.* Ithaca: Cornell University Press, 1986.

Kramer, Daniel C. *Participatory Democracy: Developing Ideals of the Political Left.* Cambridge: Schenkman, 1972.

Mansbridge, Jane J. *Beyond Adversary Democracy.* New York: Basic Books, 1980.

Rothschild, Joyce, and J. Allen Whitt. *The Cooperative Workplace.* Cambridge: Cambridge University Press, 1986.

Spiro, Melford E. *Gender and Culture: Kibbutz Women Revisited.* Durham, N.C.: Duke University Press, 1979.

Thayer, Frederick C. *An End to Hierarchy! An End to Competition! Organizing the Politics and Economics of Survival.* New York: Franklin Watts, 1973.

ARTICLES ON SMALL GROUPS AND CONSENSUAL ORGANIZATION

Ferguson, Kathy. "Toward a New Anarchism," *Contemporary Crisis* 7 (Jan. 1983): 39–57.

Gibb, Cecil A. "The Principles and Traits of Leadership," in Hare, Borgatta, and Bales, eds. *Small Groups* (New York: Alfred A. Knopf, 1961), p. 94.

Mansbridge, Jane. "Time, Emotion and Inequality: Three Problems of Participatory Groups," *Journal of Applied Behavioral Science* 9 (1973): 351–68.

Newman, Katherine. "Incipient Bureaucracy: The Development of Hierarchy in Egalitarian Organizations," in G. Britain and R. Cohen, eds. *Hierarchy in Society* (Philadelphia: Institute for the Study of Human Issues, 1980), pp. 143–64.

Rothschild-Whitt, Joyce. "The Collectivist Organization: An Alternative to Rational-Bureaucratic Models," *American Sociological Review* 44 (August 1979): 509–27.

Smith, H. Gordon. "A More Open Workplace," *Nation's Business*, May 1986.

Simmons, John, and Judy Karasik. "GM's Corporate Tuneup," *Boston Globe Magazine*, Oct. 11, 1987, p. 22.

Index

Adaptation, 9–10, 91
Aiken, Michael, 7, 10
American Woman Suffrage
  Association, 36
Anarchist feminism, 41–42
Anarchist feminist group, 117–119
Anthony, Susan B., 36, 39
Argyris, Chris, 6, 22
Authority, 15, 28

Barnard, Chester, 3, 6
Benson, J. Kenneth, 7
Blau, Peter, 17
Bureaucracy, 12–13, 46–47
Business Women's Group, analysis of
  106–107, conflicts in 111–115,
  hierarchy 107–111, 116, history,
  104–105, legislative platform 104,
  operating procedures 105–106,
  purpose, 103, structure, 105–106,
  see hierarchial organization

Capitalism, 7, 39
Carroll, Berenice, 43
Centralization, 19–20
Civil Rights Act of 1964, 104
Closed systems, 9
Coleman, James, 5, 10, see *Union
  Democracy*

Consciousness-raising groups, 37
Consensual decision making, 27–29,
  37, 120
Consensual model, 29–31
Consensual organization, compared
  with modified consensual
  (diagram), 96, defined, 27, and
  efficiency, 122, growth of, 31,
  overview 27–34, 121–122
Consensual process, 88
Consensus, 55, 59–65, 98, 119
Commission on the Status of
  Women, 37
Communication, 16, 19
Community Action, 55
Congressional Union, 36
Coordination, 16
Contingency theory, 10
Critical decision making, 76, 102n.
Critical decisions, xii, 20, 118
Critical perspective, 7, 10–12, 23–25

De-alienation, 31, 32–33
Decentralization, 19–21
Decision making, xi
Decision by consensus, xii
Democracy, 5
Democratic theory, 3, *see* Michels
Departmentalization principle, 16